Robert P. Rugel, PhD

Treating Marital Stress
Support-Based Approaches

*Pre-publication
REVIEWS...
COMMENTARIES,
EVALUATIONS...*

"*Treating Marital Stress* provides a theoretical foundation for understanding and promoting spouses' mutual support as the key mechanism for enhancing intimacy and relationship accord. Support-focused marital therapy (SFMT) promotes support across multiple domains, including emotional expressiveness, encouragement of individual goals and strengths, and strategic assistance with both individual and relationship challenges.

A notable strength of this text is its emphasis on a sequential, structured approach to achieving therapeutic goals. Each chapter begins with a specific set of therapeutic tasks, followed by detailed descriptions of clinical interventions and case examples for implementing these. This book also includes empirical findings regarding the effectiveness of SFMT in reducing couple conflicts and promoting relationship satisfaction.

The author articulates a conceptually coherent model for understanding marital distress, provides a structured series of therapist interventions and couple activities for promoting emotional and instrumental support, and includes specific strategies for addressing partners' emotional processes that interfere with relationship intimacy. Concrete clinical examples throughout the text and a detailed outcome study contribute to implementing SFMT constructs and specific clinical procedures. Both experienced couple therapists and those pursuing an initial introduction to marital therapy will find this text an invaluable resource."

Douglas K. Snyder, PhD
*Professor and Director
of Clinical Psychology Training,
Texas A&M University,
College Station*

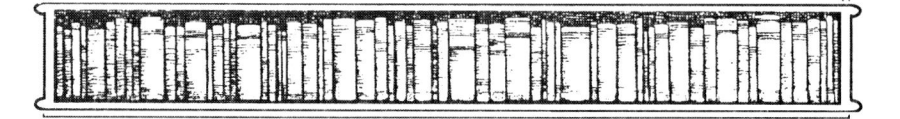

More pre-publication
REVIEWS, COMMENTARIES, EVALUATIONS . . .

"*Treating Marital Stress: Support-Based Approaches* is a very thoughtful and much-needed text that fills a gap in the field. Whereas existing treatments for couple distress typically comment on the importance of social support in intimate relationships, no other intervention approaches are built around this important aspect of couples' lives. Most forms of couple therapy focus on decreasing negative interactions, feelings, and thoughts for distressed couples. Whereas this is important, it is equally important to focus on the positive aspects of relationships, particularly social support between partners. Rugel has done an excellent job of elevating social support to the central issue around which to build interventions for distressed couples. This focus on positive factors in marriage is long overdue and greatly needed—bravo!

The book is very well written. It is clear, filled with clinical examples, and comes from someone who clearly knows and works with couples. The reader is provided with a number of specific guidelines, and the book is written as an organized treatment manual that proceeds session by session. Developing therapists will value this guidance and structure, and still there are many new ideas for the experienced therapist."

Donald H. Baucom, PhD
Professor, Director of Clinical Psychology, University of North Carolina–Chapel Hill

The Haworth Clinical Practice Press
An Imprint of The Haworth Press, Inc.
New York • London • Oxford

NOTES FOR PROFESSIONAL LIBRARIANS AND LIBRARY USERS

This is an original book title published by The Haworth Clinical Practice Press, an imprint of The Haworth Press, Inc. Unless otherwise noted in specific chapters with attribution, materials in this book have not been previously published elsewhere in any format or language.

CONSERVATION AND PRESERVATION NOTES

All books published by The Haworth Press, Inc. and its imprints are printed on certified pH neutral, acid free book grade paper. This paper meets the minimum requirements of American National Standard for Information Sciences-Permanence of Paper for Printed Material, ANSI Z39.48-1984.

Treating Marital Stress
Support-Based Approaches

HAWORTH Marriage and the Family
Terry S. Trepper, PhD
Executive Editor

The Web of Poverty: Psychosocial Perspectives by Anne-Marie Ambert

Stepfamilies: A Multi-Dimensional Perspective by Roni Berger

Clinical Applications of Bowen Family Systems Theory by Peter Titelman

Treating Children in Out-of-Home Placements by Marvin Rosen

Your Family, Inc.: Practical Tips for Building a Healthy Family Business by Ellen Frankenberg

Therapeutic Intervention with Poor, Unorganized Families: From Distress to Hope by Shlomo A. Sharlin and Michal Shamai

The Residential Youth Care Worker in Action: A Collaborative, Competency-Based Approach by Robert Bertolino and Kevin Thompson

Chinese Americans and Their Immigrant Parents: Conflict, Identity, and Values by May Paomay Tung

Together Through Thick and Thin: A Multinational Picture of Long-Term Marriages by Shlomo A. Sharlin, Florence W. Kaslow, and Helga Hammerschmidt

Developmental-Systemic Family Therapy with Adolescents by Ronald Jay Werner-Wilson

The Effect of Children on Parents, Second Edition by Anne-Marie Ambert

Couples Therapy, Second Edition by Linda Berg-Cross

Family Therapy and Mental Health: Innovations in Theory and Practice by Malcolm M. MacFarlane

How to Work with Sex Offenders: A Handbook for Criminal Justice, Human Service, and Mental Health Professionals by Rudy Flora

Marital and Sexual Lifestyles in the United States: Attitudes, Behaviors, and Relationships in Social Context by Linda P. Rouse

Psychotherapy with People in the Arts: Nurturing Creativity by Gerald Schoenewolf

Critical Incidents in Marital and Family Therapy: A Practitioner's Guide by David A. Baptiste Jr.

Family Solutions for Substance Abuse: Clinical and Counseling Approaches by Eric E. McCollum and Terry S. Trepper

Between Fathers and Sons: Critical Incident Narratives in the Development of Men's Lives by Robert J. Pellegrini and Theodore R. Sarbin

Women's Stories of Divorce at Childbirth: When the Baby Rocks the Cradle by Hilary Hoge

The Therapist's Notebook for Families: Solution-Oriented Exercises for Working with Parents, Children, and Adolescents by Bob Bertolino and Gary Schultheis

Treating Marital Stress: Support-Based Approaches by Robert P. Rugel

An Introduction to Marriage and Family Therapy by Lorna L. Hecker and Joseph L. Wetchler

Solution-Focused Brief Therapy: Its Effective Use in Agency Settings by Teri Pichot and Yvonne M. Dolan

Treating Marital Stress
Support-Based Approaches

Robert P. Rugel, PhD

The Haworth Clinical Practice Press
An Imprint of The Haworth Press, Inc.
New York • London • Oxford

Published by

The Haworth Clinical Practice Press, an imprint of The Haworth Press, Inc., 10 Alice Street, Binghamton, NY 13904-1580.

© 2003 by The Haworth Press, Inc. All rights reserved. No part of this work may be reproduced or utilized in any form or by any means, electronic or mechanical, including photocopying, microfilm, and recording, or by any information storage and retrieval system, without permission in writing from the publisher. Printed in the United States of America.

PUBLISHER'S NOTE
Identities and circumstances of individuals discussed in this book have been changed to protect confidentiality.

Cover design by Marylouise E. Doyle.

Library of Congress Cataloging-in-Publication Data

Rugel, Robert P.
   Treating marital stress : support-based approaches / Robert P. Rugel.
      p. cm.
   Includes bibliographical references and index.
   ISBN 0-7890-1631-1 (alk. paper)—ISBN 0-7890-1632-X (soft)
   1. Marital psychotherapy. I. Title.

RC488.5 .R843 2003
616.9'156—dc21

                              2002068777

For Ellen, now more than ever

ABOUT THE AUTHOR

Robert P. Rugel, PhD, is Associate Professor in the Psychology Department at George Mason University where he teaches courses in marital and family therapy. He is also in private practice in Northern Virginia. He is the author of two previous books on marital therapy: *Dealing with the Problem of Low Self-Esteem* and *Husband-Focused Marital Therapy*.

CONTENTS

Acknowledgments	xi
THE IMPORTANCE OF SUPPORT	1
Chapter 1. The Role of Support in Marriage	1
The Overwhelmed Spouse in Contemporary Marriage	1
The Literature on Social Support	2
The Five Patterns of Marital Distress	6
Specific Support-Focused Marital Therapy Interventions	9
THE TREATMENT MANUAL	13
Chapter 2. Session One: Using Empathy and Probes to Understand the Perspective of Each Partner	13
The Therapist's Goals	13
What Are Your Concerns? Working Empathically with One Spouse and Then the Other	13
What Do You Want to Achieve? Establishing a Preliminary Therapeutic Alliance with Regard to Goals	20
Describing How You Will Work Together: Establishing the Therapeutic Alliance with Regard to Tasks	22
Closing the First Session by Handling Administrative Matters	25
Chapter 3. Session Two: Processing Interactions and Presenting Patterns	27
The Therapist's Goals	27
"Processing" Conflicts and Interactions	27
Processing Mary and Pete's Conflict	28
Presenting Mary and Pete's Pattern	33
The Therapist As Relationship Instructor	35
Preparing the Couple for Individual Sessions	35

Chapter 4. Sessions Three, Four, and Five: Deepening the Therapist's Understanding Through Individual Sessions and Reorientation — 37

The Therapist's Goals — 37
Increasing the Emotional Connection — 37
Obtaining the Marital History — 38
Obtaining the Developmental History — 39
Session Five: Reorienting the Couple After the Individual Sessions — 40

Chapter 5. Working to Increase Support in Subsequent Sessions — 43

Assigning Tasks and Helping Spouses Get What They Want — 43
Understanding and Reframing the Inner Emotional Obstacles to Carrying Out Assignments — 47
Reframing the Obstacles to Providing Support — 48
Following Up on Previous Homework Assignments — 52
Identifying the Dismissive Attitude Pattern — 57
Identifying the Unilateral Attempt to Prevail Pattern: "Winning the Battle but Losing the War" — 58
Using Support Lists to Structure the Therapy Around the Issue of Support — 61
Keeping the Support Issue on the Table and Monitoring Progress — 67

Chapter 6. Dealing with Triangulation Patterns in Subsequent Sessions — 69

The Parenting Triangle — 69
Working As a Team and Problem Solving — 74
The Work or Hobby Triangle — 76

Chapter 7. Dealing with Anger Management, Derogation, and Negative Escalation in Subsequent Sessions — 83

Calming the Angry System: The Therapist As Gatekeeper — 84
Teaching the Couple to Avoid Negative Escalation — 90
Framing the Issue As Anger Management — 91

Framing Inappropriate Anger Management As a Function of Marital Deterioration	92
Dealing with the Emotional Obstacles to Anger Management and the Inhibition of Criticism	95

Chapter 8. Dealing with Communication Avoidance in Subsequent Sessions — 101

What Is Direct Communication?	101
Indirect Communication and Conflict Avoidance	101
Describing the Communication Avoidance Pattern	102
Dealing with Obstacles to Direct Communication	105

Chapter 9. Encouraging Companionship, Affection, and Sexual Intimacy in Subsequent Sessions — 109

Using the Here and Now to Enact Affectionate Behavior	109
Encouraging Companionship	111
Encouraging Nonsexual Touching and Sexual Intimacy	114

Chapter 10. Accepting Partner Differences and Limitations — 121

Differences As an Irritant	121
Learning to Accept Differences and Limitations	122
Accepting Gender Differences	124

A CASE HISTORY — 127

Chapter 11. The Marriage of Sam and Diane — 127

Introduction	127
Sessions One Through Eighteen	128
Subsequent Sessions	135

THE OUTCOME STUDY — 137

Chapter 12. Assessing the Effectiveness of Support-Focused Marital Therapy — 137

Robert P. Rugel
Jacqueline R. Shapo

Study One: The Support-Focused Marital Therapy Waitlist-Control Comparison	137
Study Two: Correlations Among Support, Anger, Marital Satisfaction, and Change in Marital Satisfaction	147

Afterword 155

References 157

Index 161

Acknowledgments

The author would like to thank the following clinical psychology graduate students who served as therapists, research coordinators, and data collectors in the Marital Therapy Project at George Mason University. Their energy, enthusiasm, and dedication to their couples made this project possible. They are Bonita Becker, Julie Borenstein, Madison DeJonge, Tanie Miller, Deborah Perlman, Mathew Picerno, Donna Marschall, Chris Sarampote, Jackie Shapo, and Jennifer White. The author would also like to thank his wife, Ellen Rugel, for her conscientious proofreading and editing of this document and for her support throughout the project. The author also thanks Robert Smith, chairman of the Psychology Department at George Mason University, for his encouragement and help. Thanks also are extended to Ralph Barocas, June Tangney, and Adam Winsler for reviewing sections of the manuscript.

THE IMPORTANCE OF SUPPORT

Chapter 1

The Role of Support in Marriage

THE OVERWHELMED SPOUSE IN CONTEMPORARY MARRIAGE

Most marriages today are under stress from the many competing obligations that spouses experience. Spouses often feel besieged as they try to meet their obligations to their children, jobs, extended family, friends, and community. Wives often feel particularly stressed. These women work during the day and often face an inequitable burden of responsibility when they return home. Husbands are often equally stressed. As has always been the case, men's self-esteem is heavily invested in their careers, and many become workaholics. However, unlike previous generations, they now feel an obligation to help at home and attend their children's school and sports activities.

When additional problems arise due to financial strain, job insecurity, problems with children, illnesses, and issues with aging parents, the stress can become overwhelming.

In the face of all these demands, it is easy for spouses to become neglectful of their relationship; yet a basic truth exists about successful marriage that is confirmed by both scientific research and common sense: *stressed-out spouses are happy in their marriages when they believe that they have the support of their partners.* Through acts of support, spouses feel accepted, valued, and loved. A lack of support causes partners to feel insignificant and diminished.

The goal of support-focused marital therapy is to increase marital satisfaction by increasing the level of social support a spouse provides to his or her partner. By social support, we mean the following:

1. *Emotional support:* the marital partner will engage in expressions of love, empathy, and concern for the spouse.
2. *Esteem support:* the marital partner will show respect for the spouse's qualities and belief in the person's abilities.
3. *Informational support:* the marital partner will help the spouse by providing factual input and advice when the spouse needs it.
4. *Instrumental support:* the marital partner will provide assistance with needs such as household and child-rearing tasks. (Cutrona, 1996)

A spouse who is on the receiving end of such support will feel loved and valued by the partner. That spouse will also know that the partner can be counted on when help is needed. As a result, security and trust develop in the relationship. The conditions are present to allow for emotional and sexual intimacy. Thus, support is a powerful factor in maintaining marital satisfaction.

THE LITERATURE ON SOCIAL SUPPORT

The following is a review of what literature tells us about the power of social support.

Social Support and Well-Being

Those who receive social support experience an enhanced sense of well-being. This has been demonstrated with a variety of populations, such as student athletes (Rosenfield and Richman, 1997), general hospital nurses (Tyler and Cushway, 1995), adolescents (Pretty et al., 1996), women during pregnancy (Zachariah, 1996), university students (Steptoe et al., 1996), community-based older adults (Steiner et al., 1996), and women diagnosed with breast cancer (Pistrang and Barker, 1995).

Cobb (1976) and Ingledew, Hardy, and Cooper (1997) have demonstrated that social support is particularly important in the presence of stress and serves to buffer individuals from the harmful effects of stress. When high levels of support are present, individuals are protected from disorders such as pregnancy complications, arthritis, asthma, and depression (Cobb, 1976).

Social Support and Self-Esteem

Social support plays a crucial role in maintaining self-esteem. DuBois et al. (1994) found that social support was a significant contributor to self-esteem, which in turn affected an individual's social adaptation. Lackovic-Grgin et al. (1996) and Short, Sandler, and Roosa (1991) found that parental and partner support correlated with higher self-esteem. Kawash and Lozeluk (1990) found that family support, defined as cohesion, was associated with higher self-esteem in adolescents.

Self-esteem is a crucial variable in understanding marital satisfaction. When a spouse's self-esteem is high, that spouse can remain nondefensive and can be open to listening to the partner's concerns or complaints. When a spouse's self-esteem is threatened, that spouse must defend his or her self-esteem by denying wrongdoing, by finding fault with the partner, and by distorting the spouse's intent.

Social Support, Self-Esteem, and Marital Quality

Support, self-esteem, and marital quality influence one another in what becomes a reciprocal cycle. Those who experience high levels of support from their spouses are more likely to be satisfied with their marriages (Franks and Stephens, 1996; Brunstein, Dangelmayer, and Schultheiss, 1996). In turn, the high quality of the marriage becomes a factor in maintaining self-esteem (Barnett and Nietzel, 1979; Murstein and Beck, 1972).

Social Undermining and Marital Dissatisfaction

When a spouse's self-esteem is threatened in marriage, the spouse becomes defensive and tends to engage in put-downs, criticism, and derogation. Vinokur, Price, and Caplan (1996) refer to this as social undermining. They suggest that social undermining consists of behaviors that display negative affect, hinder the attainment of instrumental goals, and criticize a spouse's attributes, actions, and efforts. Couples presenting for marital therapy typically experience high levels of social undermining. As stress increases in marriage, the levels of social undermining also tend to increase and contribute to marital deterioration.

Gender and Social Support

Although providing support is important to both husbands and wives, it is a more integral part of wives' socialization. Young girls are trained to be aware of and responsive to the needs of others (Jordan, 1991). As a result, women in their adult roles are named disproportionately as counselors and companions by both men and women, and as confidantes and sources of affirmation and understanding by children, spouses, and friends. Women also tend to be more involved in the tribulations of their adult children and to provide most caregiving to elderly relatives (McGrath et al., 1990).

Although husbands are also capable of offering support, less emphasis in their socialization is placed on the need to be aware of and responsive to the feelings of others. A more central aspect of husbands' socialization is the need to achieve, to become self-reliant, to be fearless, and to compete. Although these qualities may help men succeed in the world at large and may help the husband become a successful breadwinner, they do little to enhance the marital relationship.

As a result, in marriage, women often provide more support to their husbands than they receive from them (Belle, 1982). Antonucci and Akiyama (1987) report that wives receive less confiding, reassuring, respect, sick care, talk when upset, and talk about health.

The current cultural assumption of equality suggests that the level of support each spouse offers the other should be the same (Huston, 2000). This clashes with the patriarchal tradition, which promotes an inequity that favors the husband (Bloch, 1991; Ozment, 1983). Cultural shifts favoring equality have altered wives' expectations regarding the level of support they should receive from their husbands with regard to such issues as household tasks and parenting; nevertheless, wives continue to have a disproportionate amount of responsibility within the home (Bird, 1999; Greenstein, 2000). Husbands, often unwittingly, are reluctant to relinquish their patriarchal privileges within the marriage, and conflicts over expectations of support are a frequent source of marital stress (Depner and Ingersoll-Dayton, 1985; Heavey, Layne, and Christensen, 1993; Kayser, 1993).

As women have gained greater status and economic power within society, their definition of the marital relationship as one involving mutual support has become an increasingly important factor in determining their level of marital satisfaction. They expect support from their husbands and tend to view a lack of support as conscious and intentional acts of disregard. This lack of perceived support can generate self-esteem threats and anger in wives and can result in negative attributions and negative behavior toward their husbands (Bradbury and Fincham, 1990; Bradbury et al., 1996; Notarius et al., 1989).

Wives' negative behaviors create a threat to self-esteem and the need for self-protective behavior in their husbands, who, over time, become highly sensitized to their wives' accusations and anger. The result is the pattern of reciprocal negative interaction that is the hallmark of distressed marriages (Gottman, 1990, 1994).

A deteriorating marriage creates stress and dissatisfaction for both partners; however, it is proposed that it creates greater distress for wives, since they take more responsibility for maintaining the quality of the marriage and experience greater self-esteem deficits and depression when deterioration occurs (Barnett and Nietzel, 1979; Heim and Snyder, 1991; Murstein and Bec, 1972; Weissman, 1987).

Marital Therapy and Social Support

Given the strong relationship between support and marital satisfaction, one might expect that increasing the level of support that spouses provide to each other would be central to many approaches to marital therapy. However, this is not the case. Most of the major empirically based approaches to marital therapy focus on communication training, problem solving, helping partners see their spouses' underlying vulnerability and painful affect, and altering negative marital attributions and unrealistic expectations (Dunn and Schwebel, 1995). Although increased spousal support is probably a by-product of these therapies, it is not their major focus.

Support-Focused Marital Therapy

Support-focused marital therapy (SFMT) was developed to address the issue of lack of support within marriage. It uses support, gender, and self-esteem concepts to organize clinical material and guide therapist interventions. It has been influenced by the common factors literature, particularly with regard to the importance of the therapeutic alliance (Bordin, 1979; Weinberger, 1995); by emotionally focused marital therapy, with regard to the importance of describing destructive reciprocal patterns and surfacing a spouse's inner painful experience (Johnson and Greenberg, 1985; Johnson and Talitman, 1997); and by behavioral marital therapy, with regard to the importance of homework assignments and behavioral change (Jacobson and Margolin, 1979).

Lack of support occurs in five patterns of marital distress. The next section provides a description of these five patterns.

THE FIVE PATTERNS OF MARITAL DISTRESS

Pattern One: Lack of Emotional and Instrumental Support

In this common pattern, the wife presents for therapy considerably more distressed and angry than the husband. She is carrying high levels of residual anger related to the experience of lack of support and a sense of being overburdened in the relationship. In some cases the issue is lack of instrumental support. Although both may work outside the home, the marriage appears organized around the husband's activities and a real inequity exists in distribution of household tasks. Feelings of inequality and rejection build within the wife, who begins a pattern of complaining and criticizing her husband's lack of help. The husband responds by becoming defensive and withdrawn, rather than more helpful. The wife steps up her attack in what becomes a destructive cycle. A related issue is the husband's lack of emotional support. The wife feels that her husband either does not listen or is not emotionally responsive, and she subsequently feels disregarded and angry.

In a less common pattern the husband experiences lack of support and feels disregarded. In this pattern the traditional sex-role patterns are reversed. The husband is often a "people pleaser" who is eagerly supportive. The wife, despite early socialization experiences that have encouraged responding to the needs of others, is egocentric and unaware of her husband's feelings. The husband, in his desire to be supportive, often goes against his better judgment and supports his wife's unrealistic, egocentric wishes. Unexpressed resentment builds within the husband, who often becomes angry and withdrawn.

In many cases no clear asymmetry is present. Both spouses are dismissive in their mode of conflict resolution. Each attempts to resolve the clash of conflicting needs by minimizing the partner's concerns and attempting to prevail at the expense of the other. Dismissive statements that imply "I don't feel this way so you shouldn't either" characterize their interaction. Issues are repeatedly brought up for discussion and the result is a predictable argument and impasse.

Pattern Two: Triangulation

Triangulation refers to situations in which one spouse identifies as the excluded, isolated party in relationship to a third party. Husbands often experience triangulation concerning family and parenting issues. For example, wives may see their husbands as harsh disciplinarians. They feel protective of the children and thus undermine their husbands' attempts at discipline. Husbands feel that they are treated with disrespect by their wives and children and may feel excluded from family life.

Wives often experience triangulation regarding the husband's devotion to his work or leisure activities. The inner experience of the wife is "You [husband] prefer your work or hobby to me." This results in self-esteem threat and angry attacks that contribute to the negative pattern. When the relationship has deteriorated, some husbands do begin to prefer work to being with their angry partners, thus the perceived avoidance becomes real.

Pattern Three: Derogation and Negative Escalation

In this pattern the spouses are impulsive and emotionally reactive. Their interactions are characterized by interruptions, accusations, and put-downs. Their accusatory and derogatory remarks set in motion a form of reciprocal negative interaction. The partner under attack experiences a derogatory remark as a self-esteem threat and protects his or her self-esteem with a derogatory response, resulting in negative escalation. The interaction becomes damaging to the self-esteem of both.

In other couples the derogatory process is subtle. An innuendo, a sarcastic remark, a sly criticism, a negative tone of voice, or a "sour" facial expression conveys the devaluing message. Over time, a spouse's subtle suggestions, corrections, or unsolicited advice allow that spouse to remain "one up" in the relationship. The need to be "one up" predominates, creating continuous self-esteem threat for the other, who continuously finds himself or herself in the "one-down" position. The fear of being wrong, and thus "one down," becomes powerful, and spouses will go to great lengths to avoid it.

Pattern Four: Indirect Communication

In this pattern one or both spouses lack assertiveness and fail to communicate directly. One pattern involves a husband or wife who excessively seeks approval and therefore avoids possible conflict. The spouse may have self-esteem deficits and have no expectation of equal treatment in the marriage. In many cases, the spouse's need to please is so great that identifying his or her own needs is difficult.

The partners of such spouses vary. Some of the partners have similar problems, and thus both are conflict avoidant. Others are more direct and frustrated by the spouse's inability to communicate. Still others are egocentric, needy, and unable to maintain interest in others. Their obliviousness to the needs of others has preceded the marital relationship and becomes exacerbated by the partner's reticence. The accumulated resentment in the inexpressive partner results in silence, withdrawal, and passive aggressiveness.

In another pattern, spouses are distrustful and secretive. They know what they want and act on it in a clandestine manner. The underlying assumption is that others are oppositional and that if they openly express their needs, they will not get what they want. Therefore they withhold from their partners information about what they have done regarding work, travel, associates, or purchases. Eventually the partner finds out about what has been withheld and feels excluded or betrayed, thus increasing the level of suspiciousness and loss of trust in the partner.

Pattern Five: Loss of Companionship, Affection, and Intimacy

As the marriage deteriorates, once enjoyable activities diminish in frequency. The spouses no longer go for walks together, or go out to dinner or to the movies. The partners find excuses to avoid each other. They cannot find baby-sitters, are too busy with the children, or are too tired. Their schedules allow little time for togetherness.

Expressions of affection are avoided. They no longer use endearing pet names and private expressions with each other. Self-disclosure of inner experience becomes difficult. Physical gestures such as touching, hugging, or kissing are infrequent. They find excuses to avoid the intimacy of the bedroom; for example, if one or the other snores or sleeps restlessly, they may seek separate bedrooms. Weeks or months go by without sex. As the self-protective barriers solidify, spouses begin to experience the other as threatening. Intimacy feels like an invasion of personal space by an intruder.

As the vacuum grows, many spouses find others outside the marriage to meet their emotional needs, and they eventually divorce. However, some couples who reach this point remain together. Although the couple may be unhappy in the relationship, they endure. Their reasons for staying together vary. For some, marriage is utilitarian. They are uncomfortable with high levels of intimacy. It was not present in their families of origin, and they do not expect much in this regard. They married to have children, to be taken care of by a parental partner, or to achieve financial security. They are uncomfortable with too much intimacy but are also terrified of facing the world alone.

Spouses in such marriages protect themselves from the vulnerability of desire by shutting down their affectional and sexual systems. They *stop wanting* and therefore protect themselves from the pain of unfulfilled yearning.

SPECIFIC SUPPORT-FOCUSED MARITAL THERAPY INTERVENTIONS

The therapist must determine which patterns are present and which to address first. Usually, only two or three of the patterns will be addressed with a couple. Generally, the therapist will attempt to reduce the level of animosity in the relationship by addressing patterns one through four, and then address the intimacy issues in pattern five.

In order to deal with these patterns and increase support, the therapist will engage in the following interventions.

Empathic Probing to Elicit the Perspective of Each

The therapist, through empathic probing, must establish an emotional connection with each spouse. The therapist wants to understand the painful position of each spouse within the relationship and gain information about each spouse's areas of concern within the marriage. In which situations does each partner feel neglected, hurt, isolated, or frustrated? What painful emotion is elicited by the behavior of the partner in these situations? Gaining the perspective of the spouse allows that person to feel understood and safe in the therapeutic environment.

Gaining the perspective of the spouse is also important because of the information it provides to the partner. The therapist wants the partner to understand the inner world of the spouse. The therapist's empathic probing helps the partner understand more clearly what is important and what is hurtful to the spouse. Such information is crucial in altering misinterpretations and helping create a desire within the partner to become more responsive to the spouse.

Establishing the Therapeutic Alliance

The therapeutic alliance consists of the emotional bond between the therapist and spouse. It also consists of common agreement on the goals and tasks of therapy. The initial empathic probing allows the therapist to determine what each spouse wants to achieve in therapy. Does the spouse want more support, less anger, better communication, more intimacy? Maintaining a focus on the spouses' goals keeps them motivated to work in therapy.

In order to achieve these goals, the therapist and couple must agree on the tasks of therapy. In support-focused marital therapy, the spouses' tasks include bringing in relationship concerns that have arisen in the prior week, attempting to understand their repetitive patterns and how each partner contributes to them, and engaging in the homework assignments.

Providing New Information About the Partner and the Relationship

The Partner's Inner World

The therapist takes information gained from empathic probing and uses it to bring out inner emotion and unexpressed needs. For example, the therapist might say, "Your partner feels rejected and hurt when you disregard her." The therapist points out what is important to the wife. For example, the therapist might say, "This is important to your partner because spending time together means you value her company."

The therapist points out negative misinterpretations. For example, the therapist might say, "That (act) doesn't mean he doesn't love you; it simply means he has needs of his own." The therapist creates a new framework to help the spouse understand the partner differently. These reframings will often be based on gender and self-esteem concepts.

The Destructive Patterns

Spouses are often too overwhelmed by the destructive patterns to see them objectively and too self-protective to accept their contribution to them. For example, an angry wife may verbally attack her husband and then feel rejected when he withdraws, unable to see how her attack contributes to his withdrawal. A husband may ignore his wife's requests and then complain that she is angry, unable to see how his disregard contributes to her anger.

The therapist will provide an objective, third-party perspective that allows spouses to see the destructive pattern, their contribution to it, its reciprocal nature, and its negative consequences. Such information is crucial for the couple to be able to recognize the pattern and be able to say internally, "Here it is; I don't want to start down that road again."

Behavioral Tasks

Assigning Tasks

The therapist will make behavioral assignments that are intended to help the couple avoid their destructive patterns and help them achieve their goals for therapy. The assignments are related to increasing support, managing anger, detriangulating situations, communicating directly, and increasing intimacy. The therapist will describe how engaging in the suggested behavior will help the couple avoid the destructive pattern and achieve their goals for therapy. Hopefully, the spouses will engage in the suggested behavior and experience the positive results of doing so.

Exploring Obstacles to the Behavioral Assignments

Spouses often have difficulty following through with the behavioral assignments. Fears of being controlled or vulnerable are often obstacles to engaging in the assigned behavior. The therapist must examine these emotional obstacles, reframe them, and help the spouses find ways to overcome them.

Probing for the Consequences of Behavioral Assignments

The therapist will follow up with the homework assignment and assess the consequences. Did the spouses engage in the behavior? Did doing so allow them to feel better about some aspect of the relationship? If the assigned behavior did not occur, the therapist will probe for the inner emotional obstacles and attempt to help the couple overcome them.

Iteration

As the sessions continue, old issues continue to be discussed and new issues will emerge. The therapist will continue to operate in the manner described previously, seeking to elicit painful affect brought on by patterns of disregard, elaborating on the negative consequences and destructive patterns, and seeking to alter the patterns through homework assignments.

THE TREATMENT MANUAL

Chapter 2
Session One: Using Empathy and Probes to Understand the Perspective of Each Partner

THE THERAPIST'S GOALS

The therapist's goals for the first session are to

1. elicit from the spouses their experiences of the relationship and their concerns about the relationship;
2. allow each to feel that the therapist understands his or her experience and considers it to be important;
3. ascertain what the spouses' goals are in coming for treatment; and
4. convey an understanding of how the therapist and couple will work together.

WHAT ARE YOUR CONCERNS? WORKING EMPATHICALLY WITH ONE SPOUSE AND THEN THE OTHER

Empathy and empathic probing are the therapist's primary tools in session one. The therapist will begin by asking each spouse to describe his or her concerns in the marriage. The therapist's role is to work first with one spouse and then the other in order to elicit each spouse's perspective regarding the problems in the relationship. Usually, as the therapist begins to work with the spouse who initiates the discussion, the other will be content to wait his or her turn. If the other spouse is not so self-contained and begins to interrupt, the therapist must structure the therapy to stop the interruptions by clearly telling the interrupting spouse that his or her point of view will be heard as well. Indicate that little will be accomplished with interruptions. Explain that you will need to work first with the initiating partner and that you will certainly return to the other spouse to get his or her perspective.

Marital therapy, at this point, takes on the appearance of individual therapy in a conjoint setting. The therapist works individually with one, with the other observing, and then reverses the process. Taking the empathic position and delving into the perspective of each spouse will be the primary therapist task throughout the course of therapy. During the first session this means exploring the concerns that are raised initially. After the first session it also means empathic probing with regard to the concerns the couple raise about their relationship during the week preceding the therapy session.

As each new session begins, the therapist will ask, "How have things been between the two of you this past week?" When a spouse raises a concern about the relationship, the therapist will begin anew the task of working to gain an understanding of the issue from the perspective of each.

Therapist empathy serves many important purposes: (1) It is the means by which the therapist acquires an understanding of each spouse's subjective experience of the marriage. (2) It allows the partner to learn more about the inner life of the spouse, since the information disclosed through empathic probing is often information the spouse would withhold outside of the therapy room. (3) It is a means by which the therapist establishes an emotional connection with each spouse.

The value of empathy and perspective taking cannot be overemphasized. The therapist begins with empathic probing and will repeatedly return to the empathic position after other interventions.

Asking for Concrete Examples

Once the initiating spouse begins to describe a concern, the therapist will use empathic summarizing to communicate back to the spouse what is heard. For example, "So you are feeling overwhelmed and you feel that you are not getting any help," or "This project is really important to you and you feel she isn't supporting you." If the issue that is introduced remains at an abstract level, ask for a concrete example. For example, if the wife complains that the husband does not help, the therapist can say, "Can you think of examples of when you wanted help and didn't get it?"

Probing the Concrete Example Through Outward Questions

Using the example the spouse provides, the therapist can then use empathic probing to elaborate on the specific complaint. Outward questions are intended to achieve greater specificity, to broaden the context, and to learn more about the pattern. By getting the spouse to describe the events before, during, and after a problematic interaction, the therapist can begin to put together the pieces of the interactional puzzle. The therapist can assume a position of ignorance and try to fill in the missing details about who said what to whom. As the therapist listens to the material, questions will occur regarding the circumstances. For example:

Support

THERAPIST: Did you ask him to help? [Spouse replies.]
THERAPIST: So what happened then?
THERAPIST: So when he said _____, what happened next?
THERAPIST: Let's talk about who does what. What is the morning routine like? Who gets the kids ready? Who makes breakfast? What about dinner? Who gets home first?

Derogation

THERAPIST: You said she made hurtful comments. What did she say?
THERAPIST: She called you a _____ and a _____. Was there anything else?
THERAPIST: So what happened then?

Triangulation

THERAPIST: What do you mean he avoids you? What does he do?

THERAPIST: She is complaining to her mother about you. I am not sure I understand. Were they having a conversation on the phone? What did she say?

Communication Avoidance

THERAPIST: She said she wanted to do _____. You didn't want to, but didn't say anything. Then what happened?

Intimacy Avoidance

THERAPIST: So one of you goes to bed early and the other goes to bed late. Tell me how that evolved.

THERAPIST: So you sleep on the sofa and you sleep in the bedroom. Tell me how that came about.

These questions may feel intrusive; however, your job is, with sensitivity, to be intrusive in order to derive a complete picture of the circumstances surrounding the situation being discussed. Probing the concrete example will help flesh out the various issues that may be involved.

Probing Through Downward Questions

Downward questioning is intended to bring out more of the spouses' emotional experience, particularly painful affects associated with the troublesome interaction. Downward probing can broaden and deepen the way a spouse understands his or her own inner experience. It can also deepen the way the partner, who hopefully is listening, understands the spouse. For example, seeing the pain that lies behind a spouse's anger will allow the partner to see the spouse as human and vulnerable, as opposed to attacking and threatening.

Support

THERAPIST: So you ask for help and you are ignored. What does that feel like?

SPOUSE: Like I don't matter. [The therapist probes.]

Derogation

THERAPIST: What was that like for you when he said _____?
SPOUSE: I felt like he was treating me like a stupid child. [The therapist probes.]

Triangulation

THERAPIST: Tell me more about what it is like for you when you hear them talking about you.
SPOUSE: It makes me angry. [The therapist probes.]

Communication Avoidance

THERAPIST: You didn't like the idea, but you didn't say anything. What were you feeling?
SPOUSE: I didn't want to make her mad. [The therapist probes.]

Intimacy Avoidance

THERAPIST: What is it like for you sleeping on the sofa at night?
SPOUSE: It is not where I want to be. [The therapist probes.]

Conveying the Initiating Spouse's Experience to the Partner

After working with the initiating spouse, the therapist will have some understanding of what that spouse is feeling with regard to the issue at hand. It is then time to turn to the partner. In the first session, the therapist is seeking the partner's perspective on the problem the initiating spouse has presented and has not yet elicited the partner's own concerns about the problems in the relationship. The therapist might say:

THERAPIST: So in these situations she feels like she is getting no help. What is your experience in that situation?
THERAPIST: So she feels that you prefer computer games to spending time with her. What is your experience in that situation?

Eliciting and Demonstrating Equal Respect for the Spouse's Point of View

The therapist should be prepared to be immersed in the partner's perspective, and should assume that the partner's experience of the situation will be quite different. The therapist's position, which should be both explicitly stated and demonstrated, is that each spouse is equally important and each must have an equal opportunity to describe the problem from his or her own point of view. For example, a husband may reply, "I do help. She just won't admit it" or "She always asks when I am in the middle of something and then gets mad when I don't do it immediately."

The method of outward and downward questioning will proceed until the therapist is satisfied that he or she has an understanding of the partner's perspective regarding the issue. The therapist will then reflect back to the initiating spouse the therapist's understanding of the problem from the partner's perspective.

Therapist As Gatekeeper

If the spouses continue objecting to their partners' characterization of the problem and continue to interrupt, the therapist's role as gatekeeper may increase and the therapist may structure the session by talking to one and then the other. For example, a spouse may respond defensively to what is heard and interrupt with, "That is not true; you are wrong." Functioning as gatekeeper means not letting them interrupt each other and escalate their disagreement. The therapist can say:

THERAPIST: Let him finish. Then I would like to get your perspective.

When one has finished, the therapist can then turn to the other and say:

THERAPIST: How do you see this? What is your experience of this situation?

Clarifying and Holding Their Incompatible Viewpoints: Tolerating Confusion

The therapist should assume that each spouse's description of the problem will be narrow, self-serving, and full of distortions. This is human nature. More specifically, it is the result of the negative schemas, self-protective processes, and the egocentricity that characterizes spouses in distressed marriages. The spouse initiating the discussion will usually omit elements of the interaction that involve his or her own "bad" behavior. By asking each to describe his or her understanding of the problem, and by going back and forth between the partners, a more complete description of the problem and the reciprocal pattern will emerge.

After hearing each spouse's discrepant experience of the problem situation, the therapist may feel confused and begin to feel some of the hopelessness that the couple experiences. They are locked in their conflicting views of reality. One asserts that something happened and the other denies it. Each blames the other. They have repeatedly tried and failed to convince the other of the correctness of their own positions. Both are feeling misunderstood and despair at overcoming their impasse. For example, the wife says she is overburdened and her husband is selfish. The husband says that *he* is overburdened and his wife is overdemanding and never satisfied.

Each has his or her own self-protective way of constructing their marital reality. Both feel unfairly treated. Who is right? The therapist's job at this point is to contain his or her own confusion, to be open to hearing from each spouse, and to assume that, with more information, a pattern will emerge. During session one the therapist's job is simply to work at obtaining the perspective of each spouse, to elicit underlying affect, and to indicate that the perspective of each will be respected and taken seriously.

Asking the Partner to Identify Problems

The initial session may be nearly over by the time the first issue has been discussed from the perspective of each spouse. However, the session should not end before the other spouse has been given an opportunity to identify his or her own concerns about the relationship. These concerns may be unrelated to the discussion that has already transpired. Be sure that each spouse has been able to share something that he or she would like to see changed. Seeing the possibility of change is what keeps spouses working in therapy. By the end of the session, the therapist should have an idea about one or more of the issues that disturb each spouse.

WHAT DO YOU WANT TO ACHIEVE? ESTABLISHING A PRELIMINARY THERAPEUTIC ALLIANCE WITH REGARD TO GOALS

Toward the end of the first session, the therapist begins the work of establishing a therapeutic alliance. This is accomplished by focusing on the spouses' goals for therapy.

Ask the Spouses Want They Want to Accomplish in Therapy

Crucial to establishing a therapeutic alliance is determining what spouses wish to accomplish in therapy. Knowing what each wants gives the therapist direction and gives the spouses the motivation to work in therapy. Much will have been discussed and many feelings will have been stirred up during the session. By the end of the session, spouses will be in a better position to discuss what they wish to achieve. When the therapist asks, "What do you want to achieve in therapy?" the responses may be vague or concrete. If vague, the therapist must help the spouse formulate his or her goals.

Support

THERAPIST: What do you want to achieve by coming here?
WIFE: I feel that it is all on me. I don't think it is fair.
THERAPIST: So getting more help is something you want to work on in therapy?
WIFE: Yes. It isn't fair.

Derogation

THERAPIST: What do you want to achieve in therapy?
HUSBAND: She is angry all the time. I can't say a word without her blowing up!
THERAPIST: Is that something you would like to change?
HUSBAND: Yes!

Triangulation

THERAPIST: What do you want to achieve in therapy?

HUSBAND: She overprotects our son and lets him get away with murder. It has to stop!

THERAPIST: Her overprotection is something you want to change. That is important to you.

Intimacy Avoidance

THERAPIST: What do you want to accomplish in therapy?

WIFE: He is more affectionate with the dog than he is with me.

THERAPIST: You would like him to be more affectionate. Is that an important goal for you?

If what the therapist hears is consistent with what has been discussed, the formulation of goals will flow easily. As the sessions progress and the complexity of the couple's situation becomes clearer, the goals may change. Early goals tend to be obscured by subsequent goals that emerge when a more complete understanding of the marital problems is present. However, the therapist should keep the initial statement of goals in mind throughout the sessions. They are an important anchor and allow the therapist to assess where the couple began and how far they have come. If the spouses cannot identify goals, the therapist can ask them to consider at home what they want from therapy and discuss it during subsequent sessions.

Sometimes, when partners are asked what they want to accomplish in therapy, hidden agendas emerge that are inconsistent with marital therapy. For example, a spouse may say, "If it doesn't work out, I would like you to help us mediate our divorce" or "If I leave, I was hoping you could continue with my spouse in individual treatment" or "The problem is all his. I expect you to change him." The therapist will not mediate divorce or provide individual therapy. If the spouses' goals appear incompatible with marital therapy, this should be made clear to the couple and they should be referred elsewhere.

Offering Preliminary Observations About the Problems and Patterns

Although there may be confusion about the couple's problems and patterns, toward the end of session one the therapist must be prepared to give the couple some useful feedback. Based on what was heard, the therapist can give the couple some new perspective that allows them to think differently about some aspect of their relationship. If through a description of the problems and statement of the goals the therapist can clearly see that a disregard/anger or a derogation/negative escalation pattern is present, he or she should describe the pattern, how each contributes to it, and how each might work at change. The end of the first session is not too soon to begin if the pattern is clear.

If nothing is clear, the therapist can give the spouses hope by affirming that their goals for therapy are realistic and that couples usually make progress if they make a commitment to therapy and follow through. The discussion should then move on to how they will work together.

DESCRIBING HOW YOU WILL WORK TOGETHER: ESTABLISHING THE THERAPEUTIC ALLIANCE WITH REGARD TO TASKS

Establishing a therapeutic alliance also means agreement on how the therapist and couple will work toward achieving the couple's goals. The therapist must describe what he or she will do and what the spouses are expected to do.

Describing the Therapist's Role

The therapist will explain to the couple that his or her job will be to

1. try to understand what each experiences in the troublesome interactions that they report;
2. help each understand the experience of the other;
3. offer observations regarding their interactions including the reciprocal destructive patterns that are present and how each contributes to them; and
4. offer suggestions and homework assignments that will help each break the destructive patterns and help each achieve their goals for therapy.

Describing the Spouses' Roles

The therapist explains that the spouses are expected to:

1. *Bring in day-to-day concerns about the relationship.* The couple's task is to bring up relationship concerns they have had in

the intervening week. This is material that the couple and therapist will use in order to make progress. Although issues from the past may come up from time to time, the therapist will try not to become bogged down discussing them at the expense of focusing on what is happening between them now.
2. *Try to understand the perspective of the partner and respond to it.* The therapist will indicate that the spouse's task is to try to understand the inner experience of the partner, what is important to the partner, and what is hurtful. It is also to try to become more responsive to what is important to the partner.
3. *Explore their own contributions to the problems.* The therapist will explain that an additional task of spouses is to look at their own contribution to the marital problems and what they can do to change their own behavior.
4. *Follow through with homework assignments.* The couple has the task of following through with the homework assignments and discussing them in subsequent sessions.

Obtain feedback from the couple about these tasks. Do they seem reasonable? Are they consistent with or divergent from their expectations regarding marital therapy? Spouses may superficially agree but find that they have difficulty undertaking a task later on. With the exception of reporting on the events of the week, the spouses' tasks are difficult.

Discuss Commitment

Emphasize the importance of commitment. The couple's ability to persevere despite moments of frustration ultimately determines success. Indicate that progress will occur if the couple can make the commitment to come to the sessions regularly, bring up their concerns, follow through with the homework assignments, and tolerate their frustration.

Winning the Cooperation of the Reluctant Spouse

Although it is important to connect with each spouse, it is crucial to make a connection with the more reluctant spouse, usually the husband. He often comes to marital therapy unwillingly. The male spouse's socialization often puts him at a disadvantage in the marital therapy arena. He may not have the comfort level or the vocabulary he needs to describe his inner experience. He may feel uncomfortable disclosing his fears or vulnerabilities.

If the marital relationship is patriarchal, he may worry that as a result of therapy he will lose privileges, control, or respect in the relationship. He may dread exposure to his wife's anger or his own. He may believe that coming to therapy reflects a failure at handling his own problems and is an expression of weakness. He may feel inadequate during the session compared to his more verbally expressive wife.

Conveying an Understanding of Reluctance

The therapist must be particularly attuned to the feelings and perspective of the reluctant spouse. The therapist must be able to convey an understanding of the spouse's reluctance and discomfort with therapy and be able to normalize this experience. For example:

THERAPIST: I know you don't enjoy doing this. Many people would rather walk on broken glass than come to therapy. However, if you stick with it, the results will be worth it.

Establishing Goals That Encourage Involvement

Overcoming reluctance and obtaining cooperation can also be achieved by clarifying what this spouse wants to achieve through marital therapy. If the husband cannot articulate goals, the therapist can help the husband formulate his goals. For example:

THERAPIST: It sounds like you would like your wife to be less angry at you. Is this something you want to achieve in therapy?

Husbands who have not expressed this as a goal will readily agree that they want their wives to be less angry or more affectionate when this is suggested by the therapist. Identifying and working on achieving the husband's goals will keep him involved in the therapy process.

CLOSING THE FIRST SESSION BY HANDLING ADMINISTRATIVE MATTERS

At the end of the first session the therapist should indicate the need to turn to administrative matters. Discuss a time for the sessions that is mutually agreeable. Suggest that therapy works best when it becomes a reliable and predictable part of the couple's schedule. Discuss whatever obstacles might prevent regular appointments such as unreliable baby-sitters or out-of-town travel. See if these obstacles can be overcome.

Chapter 3
Session Two: Processing Interactions and Presenting Patterns

THE THERAPIST'S GOALS

The therapist has several goals for the second session. These are to

1. continue with whatever issues emerged in the first session;
2. probe for other major areas of distress in the relationship;
3. "process" conflicts and interactions;
4. convey the destructive pattern(s); and
5. make initial interventions based on the emerging patterns.

Session two begins with the therapist asking, "How did you feel about the first session?" This is a deviation from the therapist's usual method of opening the session, which is, "How were things in your relationship this week?" In this case the therapist wants feedback regarding the couple's experience of the first session. Is it what they expected? Did they get to say what they wanted to say? Did one or the other feel slighted?

Probing both partners for their experience in the first session may unearth whatever good or bad feelings spouses had about the session. If useful information emerges regarding their expectations about therapy, the therapist has an opportunity to solidify the therapeutic alliance by reviewing how they will work together. Following this, the therapist can probe for other major issues and ask about their relationship during the intervening week.

"PROCESSING" CONFLICTS AND INTERACTIONS

Processing interactions is likely to begin in session two when the couple reports on their prior week together. When the therapist asks,

"How have things been between the two of you this week?" spouses will begin describing their troublesome interactions. The troublesome situation will usually have begun when one said or did something the other experienced as nonsupportive, disregarding, angry, coercive, a put-down, harsh, etc. Sometimes the negative behavior is real, although the disrearding partner is usually unaware of its consequences. On other occasions the partner's behavior has been misinterpreted as negative. The behavior becomes a trigger for accusations, self-protective behavior, and the destructive pattern that typifies the couple's relationship. As the pattern develops, more misinterpretation, painful affect, and destructive self-protection are apparent.

Processing the interaction extends the therapist's empathic probing approach. It allows the therapist to elicit the material needed to describe the pattern and intervene to change it. It involves

1. being curious and asking questions about the situation;
2. learning more about the spouse's inner world, frustrations, painful affect, hopes, and expectations;
3. probing to unearth the spouse's perception of the partner's intent;
4. conveying the perspective of each to the other; and
5. correcting misinterpretations and misunderstandings.

PROCESSING MARY AND PETE'S CONFLICT

Consider how the therapist processes the following pattern of inequity and lack of support. Mary is usually an even tempered woman; however, she is overly responsible and can become angry when she feels overburdened. Her more intense and ambitious husband is often not focused on what needs to be done at home. Mary was initially attracted to Pete's ambitious, single minded nature. Now she sees him as selfish. Now he sees her as controlling and angry.

Mary and Pete have four boys. In the morning, Mary gets the boys fed, makes their lunches, and gets them off to the bus. In the evening she does car pooling, supervises their homework, and sees that they get to bed on time. Her boys are often willful and argumentative. She frequently becomes frustrated and harsh with them.

Pete leaves the house early and comes home late. When he is at home, he is often on the phone with clients or in front of the computer. At times he is oblivious to what is going on around him. At other times he is aware of the turmoil, but he does not intervene.

During the second session the therapist asks how things have been between them. Mary volunteers that it has been a difficult week for her.

Working with Mary

The therapist says, "Tell me more." Mary describes her frustration. She feels she gets not cooperation from her kids and no help from her husband. She finds it aggravating when they dawdle in the morning and when they refuse to do their homework in the evening.

Becoming Curious and Probing About the Circumstances: Who Does What?

Processing an interaction requires that the therapist be curious and probe. It means learning about all of the prior interactions that led to the problematic interaction. What were the circumstances? When did the interaction begin to go awry? Who said what to whom? The therapist wants to know what each spouse was experiencing. What was each intending? What was each feeling? What was misinterpreted? It requires that the therapist adopt a spirit of inquiry regarding how each experienced the troublesome interaction.

The therapist can put himself or herself in the situation and ask, "Have I ever experienced a similar situation? What was that like for me? What were the issues then?" The therapist will want to "walk around" in the interaction and see how it feels for each spouse. The therapist will ask detailed questions. What are they like in the morning? Do the children dawdle over dressing or eating? How does it feel to deal with them and the spouse? What is it like to work with them on their homework?

It turns out that the oldest child, Sammy, is the most difficult one. He pushes his parents to the limit. Mary gets angry at him and then feels guilty.

The therapist is curious about why Pete does not help his overburdened wife. The therapist temporarily switches to a focus on Pete and asks him if he helps. Pete says he does help, but if he does not meet his wife's expectations he gets criticized, so he backs off. The therapist switches the focus back to Mary and asks her about this. She agrees. She says she thinks of him as useless. Out of frustration she has excluded him from many of the routines. He now senses her constant anger in the morning and stays away.

Probing for Painful Affect

The questions lead to underlying feelings and the therapist probes for affect. How is Mary feeling at these times?

THERAPIST: It sounds like you are feeling frustrated and angry.

Mary elaborates on her frustration and anger. The therapist hears guilt. How is she feeling about herself?

THERAPIST: It sounds like you feel guilty when you lose your temper with them.

Mary agrees. At these moments she is mad at herself. The inner pain that she experiences is now more tangible to all in the session. Is Pete listening? Is he becoming aware of her painful inner experience in a way he has not understood before? The therapist hopes so and will pursue helping Pete to understand his wife's perspective later in the session when the wife's perspective is conveyed to the husband. For now, hopefully, Mary's self-disclosures are having an impact on Pete.

Unearthing Mary's Perception of Pete's Intent

How is she feeling about her husband during these situations? What does she think his intent is?

THERAPIST: What are you thinking about him at these moments?
MARY: I don't think he cares.

Mary feels she gets no help from Pete. She concludes that he is intentionally withholding and selfish. The therapist hears other feelings. She seems to be feeling alone and depressed. Therapist probing elicits that what she says to herself is: "I get no help from him. I get no cooperation from them [the children]. This is how it has always been. This is how it will always be." The result is an inner sense of loneliness and despair.

Conveying Mary's Perspective to Pete

The therapist wants Pete to understand Mary's painful inner experience. Understanding her inner pain can mobilize him to become more helpful. To facilitate this, the therapist conveys the wife's inner experience to the husband.

THERAPIST: She feels angry, overburdened, alone, sad. Did you know she felt that way?

The husband says he knows about her anger. He complains that she is always angry. The therapist pursues the issue.

THERAPIST: Yes, but were you aware of the sadness and the isolation? I think Mary feels very alone at these moments, as if no one cares. Were you aware of this?

Pete considers the information and says he was not aware of this. He looks pensive. Beyond that he does not have much to say. How much of his wife's inner world has gotten through to him? How has it affected him? The therapist does not know. As the sessions progress, hopefully the husband will understand more of his wife's inner world.

Working with Pete

The therapist begins to focus on Pete and probe for the husband's experience of the interaction.

Probing for Painful Affect

THERAPIST: Tell what it is like for you when Mary is angry.

Mary's anger causes Pete to become self-protective. In his self-protective state he is unlikely to think about what is going on internally with his wife. Pete says he withdraws when Mary gets angry. He says sometimes he would like to tell her off, but he does not. The therapist continues to probe for the husband's inner experience in the situation.

Pete sees damage being done to his kids, particularly Sammy, as a result of his wife's anger and harsh tone.

Unearthing Pete's Feelings About Mary's Intent

How does he feel about his wife? What does he think her intent is? Pete is uncomfortable with the therapist's question and evades it. The therapist persists. Pete says that, to be honest, he thinks his wife is a bully. She bullies the kids and she tries to bully him. He resents her attempts to control him. Concerns about being controlled are a frequent husband concern, just as concerns about not getting support are a frequent wife concern.

Conveying Pete's Perspective to Mary

The therapist conveys Pete's perspective to Mary.

THERAPIST: Your anger freezes him up. He thinks that you try to bully him and then he doesn't want to help. Did you know he felt this way?

Mary becomes angry and defensive. She says she is not trying to bully anybody. The therapist stays with the task of trying to convey Pete's perspective to her. The therapist agrees she is not trying to bully him, *but*, did she understand that this was *how Pete felt?* She concedes that he might feel that way; however, her defensive manner suggests that she has not absorbed much of his perspective.

Correcting Misinterpretations About Intent by Reframing

As the therapist probes and gathers information, some aspects of the pattern become clearer. To the overly responsible wife, offering to help is automatic. It is hard for her to imagine that Pete could see her trying to do several things at once and not offer to help. To her, not offering to help must be an act of intentional disregard. When this happens she becomes angry, yet she cannot see how her anger and criticism drive him further away. To Pete, Mary wants to control everything and everybody. He thinks control, not desire for help, is her motive. The therapist maintains an empathic stance with Mary by emphasizing that a goal of therapy is to help Pete become more helpful. The therapist then moves beyond the empathic position and reframes by observing that sometimes Pete's behavior is not based on intentional disregard. At times Pete is not aware that Mary needs help. On other occasions perhaps Pete does not help because he is afraid his attempts will be criticized.

The therapist suggests that Pete does not share her automatic helping orientation toward the world. Helping is not an automatic response for him the way it is for her. The therapist tries to move Mary beyond her perception that everything he does is based on intentional disregard.

The therapist maintains an empathic stance with Pete by emphasizing that a goal of therapy is that his wife be less angry with and critical of him. The therapist then moves beyond the empathic position and reframes by suggesting that there are times when Mary is not trying to control him. The therapist suggests that Mary does not get a charge out of giving orders; she just wants help and relief.

PRESENTING MARY AND PETE'S PATTERN

The pattern refers to the reciprocal negative cycle that keeps the couple stuck and unhappy. Pete does not help and Mary gets angry. Mary gets angry, so Pete withdraws and does not help. Each influences the behavior of the other and contributes to what becomes a destructive pattern.

Reciprocal destructive patterns emerge in each of the major areas of marital stress described previously. The therapist will want to

1. present the pattern;
2. reframe the pattern by emphasizing the spouse's painful inner experience within it;
3. describe how each spouse's behavior contributes to the pattern; and
4. encourage self-change in order to alter the pattern.

Identifying Mary and Pete's Pattern

When presenting the pattern, the therapist becomes an outside observer who can see the pattern objectively and offer it to the couple for their examination. The task is to help both see how they contribute to the pattern when they put the partner in a position that is painful and threatens self-esteem. Pete does this by not helping, causing Mary to feel intentionally disregarded. Mary does it through anger and accusations, causing Pete to feel unworthy and inadequate.

THERAPIST: [To Mary] You feel you get no help and that he doesn't care about your situation. Then you become angry and attacking.

THERAPIST: [To Pete] You feel unfairly attacked so you defend yourself. You argue, nothing changes, and you both feel stuck and angry.

THERAPIST: So the pattern goes like this: You don't help. She gets angry. You avoid her. Then she gets angrier. We have to change this pattern.

Bringing Out Painful Affect and Suggesting Self-Change

The therapist probes for underlying painful affect in order for them to understand how their behavior inadvertently inflicts pain on the other. Pete needs to know how it feels to Mary when she feels overburdened, ignored, and alone in the relationship.

THERAPIST: [To Pete] Mary feels that if you don't want to help her, you must not care about her. That hurts her. Then she becomes angry and attacking. If you helped her, she would feel cared for and valued and she would be less angry with you.

The therapist makes a similar attempt to help Mary understand how it feels when Pete is the recipient of her unpredictable anger.

THERAPIST: [To Mary] When you accuse Pete of being selfish, he feels he is being told he has no value as a person. That hurts. So he defends himself instead of becoming more helpful. You need to work on becoming less attacking.

Coming from a Position of Concern When Describing the Spouse's Contribution

No new understanding will be achieved if the spouse feels blamed for the problem. The therapist, in describing the contribution a spouse makes to the destructive pattern, must come from a position of *concern* and a desire to be *helpful*. The therapist must watch for accusatory or judgmental attitudes that can creep into the presentation of a spouse's contribution to the pattern. The intent is not to blame anyone; instead, it is to open a spouse's eyes to the situation and what each spouse is inadvertently doing to the other.

Describing the Behavior As Inadvertent

The therapist can use phrases to imply that their destructive behavior is often inadvertent and therefore reduce blame.

THERAPIST: I don't think you are aware that Mary feels rejected when you don't offer to help.

THERAPIST: You *inadvertently* rejected her by not pitching in. I don't think you have done this intentionally.

THERAPIST: I think what you did was *unintentional;* however, it had these consequences. She felt ignored and unimportant.

THERAPIST: I think you did that out of *frustration*. I don't think you intended to be hurtful, but when you said Pete was selfish, he was hurt.

THE THERAPIST AS RELATIONSHIP INSTRUCTOR

In processing interactions and presenting the pattern, the therapist must function as a concerned, empathic, relationship instructor. The therapist's job is to help the spouse become aware of the relationship dimension, i.e., aware of his or her own behavior and how it creates a painful inner experience for the partner.

Processing conflicts and presenting the pattern leads to suggestions and homework assignments designed to alter the destructive pattern. The suggestions and assignments that flow from descriptions of the pattern will be discussed in the chapters that follow.

PREPARING THE COUPLE FOR INDIVIDUAL SESSIONS

As the second session comes to an end, the therapist has captured each spouse's perspective, processed material, conveyed at least a rudimentary understanding of a destructive pattern, and discussed how each might change to improve the relationship.

The therapist's final task during session two is to explain to the couple that the next two sessions will be individual sessions. In order to better understand them as individuals, the therapist would like to get their personal histories and also would like to hear more about their experience of the marriage.

Chapter 4

Sessions Three, Four, and Five: Deepening the Therapist's Understanding Through Individual Sessions and Reorientation

THE THERAPIST'S GOALS

During the individual sessions the therapist has the following goals:

1. to increase the emotional connection between therapist and spouse, thus improving the working alliance;
2. to understand the history of the marriage from the perspective of each spouse;
3. to gain information about each spouse's personal history, thus allowing the therapist to understand each spouse better as an individual;
4. to gather more information about how to intervene; and
5. to reorient the couple.

INCREASING THE EMOTIONAL CONNECTION

There is no substitute for the individual session when attempting to establish an emotional connection with each spouse. The individual session is similar to the private time a child spends with a parent. With no other "siblings" present, this time has a nurturing component that is not felt during in the tension-filled conjoint session.

In conjoint sessions, threatened spouses can make a variety of hostile, bullying, and hurtful remarks that can generate feelings of dislike or disgust in the therapist. Spouses appear more human and vulnerable in the individual sessions. The individual history-taking sessions allow the therapist to "get behind" those noxious behaviors and understand the difficult events in each spouse's developmental history that predispose the spouse to engage in abrasive behavior. Such knowledge will enable the therapist to feel less judgmental of the spouse in future sessions. Showing interest in the spouse's marital and personal history will allow the spouse to feel understood and accepted in a way that is not possible in the presence of the partner.

OBTAINING THE MARITAL HISTORY

Usually there is no explicit discussion of confidentiality regarding the material obtained in the individual session. The working assumption is that material discussed in an individual session will be revealed only if both spouses have prior knowledge of it. Secrets, such as undisclosed affairs, will not be shared. If secret material emerges in the individual session, the issue of confidentiality should be raised at that time and the therapist should make clear that this information will not be disclosed.

The first half of the individual session should be devoted to obtaining the marital history. Inquire about the following:

- How did the couple meet?
- What did the spouse find attractive in the partner?

Spouses are often attracted to a partner who is different, who fills in a missing aspect of the self, and who counterbalances the spouse's own troublesome tendencies in some way. The therapist can look for the following: Did the spouse choose a partner who would protect him or her? Did the spouse choose a partner whose deficiencies would permit a feeling of being "one up" in the relationship? Did the spouse's choice involve security over passion?

Over time, spouses begin to resent the same characteristics that initially attracted them. Being protected once felt good, but now feels suffocating. The partner's deficiencies that allowed a spouse to feel "one up" now are a source of lack of respect. The lack of passion that created security now seems boring. Gaining information about the initial attraction can be useful in helping spouses accept their partners' differences and limitations.

The therapist will want to know when the marital problems began. To determine this the following will be asked:

- How were the early years of dating and marriage?
- How was their sexual relationship?
- What were relationships like with extended family?
- What happened around developmental transitions such as the birth of children, job changes, or going back to work?
- What seemed to exacerbate the problems?

Obtaining each spouse's perception of the marital history allows the therapist to gather information about what specific events appear to have triggered the marital problems. Such information can be incorporated into the therapist's formulation of the couple's problems.

The therapist should also use the session to clarify the spouses' goals for therapy. How would each like the marriage to be different? What would each like to accomplish?

OBTAINING THE DEVELOPMENTAL HISTORY

After taking the marital history, the therapist should turn to the developmental history. The therapist may want to say something such as, "I know more could be covered, but we are going to switch gears now and get your personal history. One way to start is to get your earliest memories." This question usually is unsettling. However, it moves spouses away from telling a "prepackaged" story of their personal history that may exclude important information. Another opening might be, "Tell about your early years, before you entered school."

The therapist wants to know how this person has coped with life as an individual. How successful was this person in developing the skills necessary to function in the world of work and in the world of relationships? What occurred in the family of origin that could shed light on the spouse's current level of adjustment? What difficulties or traumas did this person have to cope with as a child? Were each spouse's security and emotional needs met as a child? Were power struggles the only mode of conflict resolution in the family of origin? Were patterns of derogation present? How has this influenced the choice of the partner and influenced the destructive patterns in the marital relationship?

The therapist should obtain information about each developmental period in each spouse's life: the preschool years, elementary school, intermediate and high school, and young adulthood. Information should also be collected regarding the following:

1. The family of origin. What were relationships like with parents, siblings, extended family (the presence of grandparents, uncles, aunts)?
2. The presence of trauma, illnesses, or disabilities with the spouse or other family members.
3. Geographic moves.
4. A chronology of academic and work experiences.
5. A chronology of dating and sexual history.
6. A chronology of alcohol and drug history.
7. A chronology of medical history.
8. An assessment of the spouse's self-concept, self-esteem, coping strategies, and self-protective processes.

Because time is limited, the therapist must try not to get bogged down with any one aspect of the history. If the spouse appears to focus too heavily on one phase, the therapist can say something to move the process forward, such as, "I wish we could spend more time on this, but we need to cover other areas."

At the end of the interview, the emotional bond between therapist and spouse should be strengthened. This bond can serve as a buffer during difficult moments between the therapist and spouse later in the therapy. In addition, the information that has been gathered should give the therapist a clearer notion of how to proceed.

SESSION FIVE: REORIENTING THE COUPLE AFTER THE INDIVIDUAL SESSIONS

The beginning of session five will often feel somewhat unfocused. The therapist will not have seen the couple together for three weeks or more and may have lost a sense of what is happening in their day-to-day interactions. The spouses may be uncertain about what the therapist will do with the material that was gathered in the individual sessions. The therapist may or may not choose to use that material to make a more formal presentation of the problems and destructive patterns in the relationship.

If the therapist feels that the therapy is unfocused and that a formal presentation will create needed structure, he or she can present the formulation of the problems in their relationship in a didactic way. This provides another opportunity to describe the problems, how each has contributed to them, and what each can do to improve the relationship.

The therapist may choose to make a chronological presentation by discussing the first emergence of problems at a particular stage in their relationship and then indicate the occurrence of other problems as they emerged. What they face now and how these problems can be addressed in therapy can then be described.

An alternate approach is to describe the current areas of distress such as lack of support or triangulation without reference to the past. Regardless of the approach, the therapist must be careful not to inundate the couple with too much information. A piece of the case formulation should be presented and then the therapist should seek feedback from the couple about it. After processing one piece of the case formulation, another piece of information can be introduced and processed.

If the therapist has already presented patterns and assignments in earlier sessions and believes a formal presentation is not necessary, the couple must be reoriented to one of their major tasks, which is to bring up their concerns about what is currently happening in their relationship. The therapist can begin the session by saying, "It was quite helpful to me to get your personal histories; now I would like to hear what your relationship has been like since we last met." The therapist will then focus on what they report and on the previous issues and assignments.

Chapter 5

Working to Increase Support in Subsequent Sessions

In this chapter we will consider how the therapist deals with the support issue in subsequent sessions. Assigning support-related homework, providing a rationale for the homework, dealing with obstacles to homework completion, following through, and processing successes and failures are the crux of support-focused marital therapy.

ASSIGNING TASKS AND HELPING SPOUSES GET WHAT THEY WANT

Homework assignments emerge from the description of the destructive pattern and the therapist's attempt to help the spouse develop prosocial behavior that will alter it. The therapist suggests that the destructive pattern is brought about, in part, by the spouse's own behavior X, which elicits painful affect and prompts self-protective behavior on the part of the partner. The therapist suggests that the spouses can improve the quality of the relationship and get what they want by reducing the frequency of objectionable behavior X and replacing it with constructive behavior A. Let us consider this with respect to the support issue.

The "What Can I Do to Help?" Assignment

The overall goal of support-focused marital therapy is to help spouses discern what is important to their partners and respond to it. This will result in a wide variety of support-related assignments. When the lack-of-support pattern is present, nearly universal is the

"What can I do to help?" assignment. In a variety of troublesome situations in which the wife is obviously angry and distressed, the husband will be encouraged to ask what he can do to help (or will be asked to figure it out without posing the question).

Providing a Rationale for the Helping

As important as the assignment itself is the accompanying rationale that puts the assignment in the context of the destructive pattern. In making the assignment, the therapist describes the destructive pattern, the reservoir of anger the wife carries as a result of lack of help, and the husband's sense of feeling besieged with his wife's anger. He explains how the assigned behavior will help alter the pattern.

The therapist can use gender differences as part of the rationale. For example, the therapist might say:

THERAPIST: [To Pete] Thirty years ago roles were more rigidly defined. Her job was to take care of the house and kids and yours was to go to work. Now she has two jobs. She goes to work and has work pressure, as do you. I think you are both under a lot of pressure at work. She comes home and has a second pressure: the house and kids. You may feel that pressure too, but it is more intense for her. She has been trained to worry about these things in a way that you haven't. When you walk into the house, you are better able to relax; the work day feels over. She can't. Her core sense of self is tied up in the appearance of the house, whether the kids are going to have a nutritious dinner, whether they are going to do their homework, whether they get to sleep at a decent hour, how they are doing in school, how they are feeling about themselves. If these things are well taken care of, she feels she has failed as a mother. Her self-worth is on the line at home in a way that yours isn't. These things are crucial to her. When you don't help with them, she feels unsupported and becomes angry.

"Relationship Monitoring" Activities

As "relationship monitors," wives are constantly investing mental energy in monitoring the emotional well-being of those around them. This adds to their experience of burden. The therapist can explain this to the husband:

THERAPIST: [To Pete] When you sit down to read the paper, it is likely you can concentrate on the paper. When she sits down to read the paper, she is also wondering if you [husband] are all right, or is there something she could be doing for you? Are the children all right, or is there something she could be doing for them? Is her sister all right, or should she call her? The neighbor just had surgery. Should she make dinner and bring it over?

The therapist describes to the husband how women are rarely off duty. As a result of their socialization, they are constantly thinking about what they could be doing for others. When roles were rigidly defined, this was a major expectation. Now it is added to their work-related responsibilities. As a result, the inner burden that they carry around is great. The therapist wants Pete to understand this about Mary. Increased understanding provides the rationale for helping.

THERAPIST: [To Pete] If you can be more supportive, I think she will feel less rejected and be less angry. In the evening if you were to say, "Is there anything I can do to help?" and then be prepared to do what she asks, I think there would be less tension. Can you see yourself doing this?

The "Monitor and Edit Your Anger" Assignment

The equivalent assignment for Mary is the "monitor and control your anger" assignment. Wives often experience moralistic rage as a result of the unfair burden that they feel they carry. The therapist wants the wife to understand that it damages the relationship when she loses control of her anger. Her anger inevitably makes her husband defensive and contributes to the destructive pattern. Although the therapist works to reduce the wife's anger by helping the husband become more supportive, the wife also must work on anger management.

THERAPIST: [To Mary] If you can work at not losing control of your anger and attacking him, I think he will be less defensive and more open to helping. When he feels attacked, he freezes and can't think clearly. Then he withdraws.

The Coordinated Homework Assignment

Often, homework assignments are coordinated so that each partner is working simultaneously at altering the reciprocal destructive pattern. In the previous example, the coordinated assignment is intended to alter the impasse created by lack of support and high levels of anger. The therapist says to the husband, "Be more helpful." The wife is told, "Monitor and control your anger." The assignments make clear how the pattern is reciprocal, what role each plays in it, and how each can change it.

Identifying Homework Assignments That Have Payoffs and Can Result in Corrective Emotional Experiences

In formulating an assignment for Pete, the therapist must make clear that although the assignment is directed toward an expressed need of his wife (support), doing so will pay off for him as well (Mary will be less angry). Initially the spouses will work at the assignments if they trust the therapist's judgment and understand the rationale. If spouses subsequently see that their efforts pay off, they will continue to engage in the behavior without the urging of the therapist.

The successful completion of a homework task and discussion of that success during the sessions provides the basis for a corrective emotional experience. The receiving spouses will begin to *experience* their partners as more responsive. The initiating partners will *experience* that they are capable of reducing stress in the relationship by engaging in the supportive behavior.

Avoiding Trivial Assignments

It is better to give no assignment at all than to give an assignment that misses the mark. The therapist must avoid the tendency to create trivial homework assignments simply because an assignment should be made. The therapist must wait until the couple's interaction has been "processed" sufficiently and the pattern is understood. Giving an assignment that is off the mark undermines the couple's faith in the therapist.

Dealing with the Overriding Spouse or the Tangential Spouse When Making an Assignment

Spouses who are poor listeners will override the therapist, just as they do the partner. When the therapist presents the pattern and the rationale for the assignment, the spouse will ignore the therapist and respond tangentially, for example, by presenting a related grievance. The therapist needs to be aware when feedback is being ignored and bring the spouse's attention back to the issue. The therapist needs to stop the interaction by saying something such as to the following to the spouse:

THERAPIST: A minute ago I suggested that you could avoid this problem if you considered doing X. What are your thoughts about this?

UNDERSTANDING AND REFRAMING THE INNER EMOTIONAL OBSTACLES TO CARRYING OUT ASSIGNMENTS

Most spouses feel victimized by their partners' bad behavior and believe that *the partner should change.* This unwillingness to accept responsibility is an obstacle to working on self-change assignments. The therapist can empathize with the spouse who resents being asked to change. The therapist can agree that the partner may need to change and will be working in therapy to do so. However, the therapist can offer a "pragmatic reframing" to deal with the spouse's resistance to the assignment by pointing out that the spouse's own behavior blocks his or her partner from changing. The therapist must help such spouses to see that altering their own behavior will help them achieve their own goals for therapy.

In addition to the general belief that the partner should change, a variety of fears, rigidities, and external stressors serve as obstacles to spouses following through with assignments. Inertia, fear of being controlled, resistance to loss of freedom, feeling unfairly burdened, defensiveness, egocentricity, and fear of unending demands may all interfere with the successful completion of assignments.

Anticipating Obstacles

The therapist must anticipate these emotional obstacles and be prepared to deal with them. When suggesting a homework assignment, the therapist should "walk through it" in advance to determine what obstacles might be present. For example, the therapist might suggest a support-related assignment and then say to Pete, "What might get in the way of your doing this? Is it possible that you will feel controlled and resent this?" If Pete can explore his inner experience and recognize the emotional obstacle (fear of being controlled), he and the therapist can discuss it.

REFRAMING THE OBSTACLES TO PROVIDING SUPPORT

The therapist's approach to obstacles is to use reframing to reduce their intensity. Reframing requires that the therapist provide the spouse with a new perspective that reduces fear and encourages the spouse to take the risk and engage in the supportive behavior.

Following are some of the typical inner emotional obstacles that may be present when a spouse is asked to become more supportive.

Inertia and Resistance to Change

Some husbands are not attuned to the support issue. They fail to identify situations that call for support and are startled by their wives' sudden explosive anger. After a single discussion of the support issue, the wife may unrealistically assume that the husband now understands the issue completely. His subsequent lapses in providing support may again seem to her to be intentional disregard. The therapist must reduce the wife's belief that she is being intentionally disregarded in such instances.

The therapist can reframe the husband's failure to follow through with support assignments as an example of inertia. Inertia refers to the natural resistance to changing one's behavior since doing so involves effort and discomfort. Because of the power of inertia, many failures to carry out assignments will occur. The therapist expects that the process will involve progress and relapse; there often will be "two steps forward and then one step back."

THERAPIST: [To Mary] Pete doesn't yet understand. He doesn't intend to be hurtful. He just hasn't yet "gotten it." This takes time.

THERAPIST: [To Pete] I think it is difficult to make these changes. It doesn't feel natural and sometimes you will slip. I don't think you intend to reject her; however, inadvertently this is what happens when you forget to be supportive.

If this reframing has the effect of calming Mary, and if Pete begins to overcome inertia and "get it," Mary's perception of intentional disregard will diminish.

Fear of Being Controlled

Pete may become resistant because he interprets the request to be more supportive as controlling.

Probing Pete's Fear in Order to Understand It

Consider this example. Pete has resisted coming home on time for dinner and does not call when he will be late. This has been a source of many arguments. The therapist wants to understand clearly what this issue is about for Pete so that it can be accurately reframed. As the therapist probes and discusses the issue with Pete, it becomes clear that coming home on time means restricting his freedom. Stopping in the middle of a project at work is frustrating. He is not accustomed to having his freedom of movement curtailed.

Pete also resists calling home. As the therapist probes, it appears that calling home when he will be late feels controlling and demeaning to Pete. It is similar to reporting to his mother.

Reframing Fears of Control

In an attempt to neutralize Pete's fear of being controlled, the therapist reframes Mary's intent by suggesting that her request comes not from a desire to control him but, instead, from her desire for evidence that he cares about family life.

THERAPIST: [To Pete] I know it feels as if she is trying to control you when she asks you to do this, but for her this is about wanting to know she and the kids count. If you come home for dinner on time, she feels as though she means something to you. She isn't into being the drill sergeant and giving orders. That doesn't do anything for her. To her, your coming home on time is about feeling cared about.

Pete is *afraid* of being controlled. If the therapist's reframing is effective, Pete may see Mary's request differently. The request may indeed control him. He must let go of his work in order to be home on time. However, the therapist has attempted to reinterpret Mary's *intent*. The therapist suggests that, for Mary, the issue is about allowing her to feel important in the relationship. If Pete can understand his wife in this way, take the risk, come home on time, and experience decreased tension in the relationship, his fear of being controlled may diminish.

Fears of Being Overburdened

Pete may be highly stressed with his job and home responsibilities. He may resist becoming more supportive because he believes that he does more than his share. He may feel that the therapist fails to understand his plight as the already overburdened partner.

Probing Pete's Sense of Being Burdened

The therapist will want to explore Pete's sense of feeling overwhelmed and resentful. It is important to know about all of the stresses and burdens Pete experiences at work and to understand Pete's belief that when he comes home he should be able to relax. This information can help the therapist in reframing.

Reframing Pete's Resistance to Helping

THERAPIST: [To Pete] I know you already feel overburdened. I think you are under a lot of stress with your job. I want your wife to appreciate what you go through at work. If you help her with the kids, in the long run it will be easier on you. You will be free from arguing about it all the time. I think you will feel less burdened.

The overstressed husband is *afraid* of increasing his load and losing his "downtime." If the reframing is effective, it will provide him with a rationale for taking the risk of engaging in the proposed supportive behavior. If a decease in arguing is the result, his fear of being overburdened will diminish.

Defensiveness

Mary described the following repetitive pattern. When she would try to have a conversation with Pete, he would get distracted and interrupt the conversation by making phone calls. At such moments Mary felt rejected and angry. She would make accusations and Pete would get defensive.

Probing for Pete's Inner Experience

Probing Pete's inner experience revealed that Mary's attack left him feeling worthless. This led to attempts to defend himself and to escalating arguments. The therapist pointed out Mary's need for his attention and the damage caused by his inattentiveness. This was identified as a problem to be addressed; however, the therapist wanted to find a way to protect Pete from self-recrimination and defensiveness.

THERAPIST: [To Pete] Mary has been raised to be attentive to others. She does this automatically.

The therapist checked with Mary for confirmation then returned to Pete and said:

THERAPIST: You haven't been raised that way. In your family, you didn't learn how to be attentive to others. Sometimes men have to go through on-the-job training to learn to be more attentive. When you slip and forget, it doesn't make you a bad person. You just had a lapse. Don't condemn yourself!

Fear of Disappointment

After years of offering support and getting nothing in return, some spouses are afraid to resume supportive behavior. It means once again risking disappointment. Although spouses want the relationship to improve, they are unwilling to take the risk and become supportive again.

THERAPIST: [To Mary] I know that you have been disappointed many times. Now you are afraid to try because you my be disappointed again. But you need to take the risk. Otherwise you remain stuck.

FOLLOWING UP ON PREVIOUS HOMEWORK ASSIGNMENTS

Remaining Objective About What Has Occurred

A typical therapy session begins by asking the couple about how their relationship has been in the intervening week. If what emerges is unrelated to a previous homework assignment, the therapist will first process this new material, then inquire about what has transpired with regard to the homework. *Do not assume that they have done their homework.* The emotional obstacles, particularly in the beginning, may prove too great. The therapist must be open to processing whatever *has* occurred. Both successful and unsuccessful homework assignments are "grist for the mill" and allow the therapist to learn how the couple interacts.

THERAPIST: [To Pete] Tell me what happened with regard to helping. Did you ask, "What can I do to help?"

THERAPIST: [To Mary] Were you able to refrain from criticizing Pete?

How did Pete handle the helping assignment? Did he try to do it? Did he forget to do it? Did he get distracted? Did they argue about it? Did they decide it was not important? Did they do something else instead? How did Mary handle the "refrain from criticism" assignment? Was it on her mind? Was she successful in editing her comments?

Focusing on the Consequences of a Successful Homework Assignment

If the assigned supportive behavior did occur, the therapist must probe to understand its consequences.

Corrective Emotional Experiences for the Initiating Spouse: Learning Prosocial Control

Sometimes the consequences of the supportive act have been obvious. Mary has been visibly appreciative and Pete is aware of this. In other instances, the therapist needs to unearth information from Mary that allows Pete to see the positive consequences of his behavior. By probing and unearthing positive feelings in Mary, the therapist brings out the information Pete needs to develop his own rationale for helping.

THERAPIST: [To Mary] So he did say, "What can I do to help?" and then followed through? What was that like for you?

The therapist probes for evidence that the recipient appreciated the effort.

MARY: I appreciated it.
THERAPIST: Tell me more.

The therapist probes Mary's inner experience so that the meaning of the supportive act becomes clearer to Pete.

MARY: I felt like he was aware of what I was dealing with. It was also a relief to have help.
THERAPIST: That is great. [Expanding on the issue] Did you feel less alone?
MARY: A little bit.

Disconfirming Pete's Fear of Being Controlled

The therapist's empathic probing should also focus on whatever occurred within Pete. It may be that he did not feel controlled when engaging in supportive behavior.

THERAPIST: [To Pete] You were able to say, "What can I do to help?" What was that like for you? Did you feel controlled?

The therapist probes for evidence that Pete found engaging in the behavior harder or easier than expected.

The Ultimate Goal: Perception of the Partner As Responsive

Spouses who are the recipients of supportive behavior also have the opportunity for a corrective emotional experience. They can experience that their partners are aware of and responsive to their concerns. Although Pete initiates the supportive behavior at the urging of the therapist, if he develops his own rationale for doing so and becomes reliable in offering support, Mary's perception of him as responsive may undergo a more permanent change. This is the ultimate goal of support-focused marital therapy.

Probing for Inhibition of Noxious Behavior: Making Covert Behavior Overt

In cases where the spouse is asked to inhibit negative behavior, carrying through with the assignment means engaging in self-control and *not* doing something. When a wife is successful in inhibiting criticism, the occasion may go unnoticed by the husband, who has no knowledge of the wife's successful inner struggle. In their daily lives it is unwise for the spouse to say, "I just inhibited a critical remark." Although this may be counterproductive at home, such instances should be discussed in the therapy session. The therapist must probe to make such private efforts at self-control overt. For example, the therapist will say to Mary:

THERAPIST: Have you been trying not to be critical of Pete this past week?

Such probing may allow the spouse to discuss successful, but private, efforts to inhibit noxious behavior. By making these covert efforts overt, Pete can see that Mary is working to improve the relationship.

Instances in Which the Supportive Behavior Is Carried Out and Has No Positive Consequences for the Recipient

In many distressed marriages spouses are unwilling to "let the partner off the hook" when the partner successfully engages in supportive behavior. One positive act does not erase years of disappointment. The spouse remains distrustful. In such instances the therapist must take the empathic position with the distrustful spouse. The therapist might say:

THERAPIST: Was he more helpful?
MARY: Yeah. He has been this way before. It never lasts.
THERAPIST: You feel that one helpful act doesn't suddenly wipe the slate clean. Because he was helpful today doesn't mean it will happen tomorrow.

Following the empathic response, the therapist must probe for anything positive that the spouse may have experienced as a result of the helpful act.

THERAPIST: I know you are still distrustful, but did it relieve your burden somewhat?

With probing, Mary may grudgingly acknowledge that the behavior was helpful.

If the recipient of support expresses no appreciation when a successful homework assignment is carried out, the therapist may need to deal with the initiating spouse's anger. Feeling unappreciated, and also looking for an excuse not to engage in the recommended behavior, the initiator may respond, "You see? Why bother? Nothing is going to change!" The therapist must empathically acknowledge the initiator's frustration and point out the need for patience.

THERAPIST: I know this is frustrating. Marital therapy takes time. I am glad you were more helpful. Even if she is not appreciative, you should feel better about yourself. Keep at it.

Processing Failures to Carry Out Assignments

The Failed Assignment Based on Inertia—Try Again

A discussion led to agreement that Pete would plan an activity that they would do together, thereby relieving Mary of the burden. Since this was a highly infrequent act for Pete, inertia could be an obstacle. Sure enough, at the next session, he revealed that he had not done it. The therapist suggested that changing old patterns was hard and then repeated the rationale for the assignment: doing so would allow his wife to feel he was thinking about their relationship. The therapist suggested that he try again.

Halfhearted Compliance—A Good First Step

The initial support assignments often result in halfhearted compliance. For example, Pete may be resentful and still believe that his wife should change. He does the assigned supportive behavior once or twice and then forgets. The therapist asks, "How did it go with respect to helping?" Mary remains angry. She says, "He helped, but then he stopped." Similarly, Mary may find it difficult to edit out her angry, critical responses. She may feel Pete's behavior warrants criticism.

The therapist must process such halfhearted attempts for the inner experience of each spouse. What was the experience of each on the successful and unsuccessful days? What were the payoffs on the days when he did help? What were the obstacles on the days when he did not? Processing the successes and failures allows the therapist to repeatedly present the destructive pattern and provide the rationale for the assignment. Halfhearted compliance is a good first step.

A Failed Assignment That Is Good Grist for the Mill

During a session, Mary requested that Pete change the oil in her car. The therapist agreed that this would be a good step toward working together as a couple. Pete agreed to do so.

At the next session they report that Pete has not done the assignment. The therapist processed the interaction. It appeared that Pete did not have time over the weekend to accomplish all the tasks he had planned, and he asked Mary to help him by buying an oil filter. Mary (still angry over other matters) refused. Pete became infuriated and refused to change the oil. A power struggle ensued.

Although the assignment failed, it provided the therapist the opportunity to further explore their relationship. What was going on within Mary that blocked her desire to be helpful? What does Pete experience when she is uncooperative? How did this ultimately become a power struggle? The failed assignment became an opportunity for the therapist to gain a deeper understanding of their destructive pattern.

Refining an Assignment That Backfired

After eliciting Mary's feelings of being ignored, the therapist suggested that Pete ask Mary about her day. Pete followed through and did so; however, the assignment backfired. When she began to describe her day, he appeared bored and impatient. She felt rejected and exploded in anger.

Therapist probing revealed that Pete experienced his wife's recitation of her day as long and overly detailed. It contributed to his poor listening.

The therapist inquired about how long Pete thought he was capable of listening before he would become impatient. The therapist probed to determine if Mary knew when she went on too long. The homework assignment was refined and became a coordinated task. Pete would listen to Mary, try to be patient, and indicate when he had reached his threshold. Mary would work on covering the highlights of her day and editing out the details.

IDENTIFYING THE DISMISSIVE ATTITUDE PATTERN

Marital distress is often triggered by a spouse's *dismissive attitude*. When there is a clash of needs, some spouses try to prevail in the conflict by dismissing the importance of the partner's requests, feelings, or opinions. Their approach is, "I don't feel that way, so you should not feel that way either." The implicit thinking is, "This issue is not important to me, and dealing with it causes me inconvenience; therefore, it should not be important to you." The spouse expresses to the partner some variation of the following:

- Why do you get so upset about this? You are making a big deal out of nothing.
- I don't feel this way; you shouldn't either.
- This doesn't bother me; therefore, it shouldn't bother you.
- I don't go around wanting this, so you shouldn't either.
- Why can't you relax about this? Chill out; it is no big deal. You are getting upset about nothing.

Consider the following example. Pete and Mary have discussed a housekeeping issue. Keeping a clean house is extremely important to Mary. In this instance, she expresses her unhappiness with her husband's unreliability in taking out the trash on "trash days."

As they discuss the issue, Pete's response to her request is dismissive. He says, "It will get taken out sooner or later. It is no big deal." Pete's dismissive attitude hurts Mary, who feels disregarded. She then escalates the argument by exaggerating her complaints. She says, "You never take out the trash. You always find excuses." Her exaggerations give Pete an opening to defend himself. He says, "That is not true; I do take out the trash, just not when you want me to." This results in further escalation of their argument.

The therapist needs to point out the dismissive attitude and reorient Pete. Pete is thinking, "This is no big deal." He needs to be thinking some variation of the following:

- This is not that important to me and doing it is inconvenient. However, she is different. Apparently, it is important to her.
- Although I don't completely understand why this is so important to her, undoubtedly it is.
- Although I find it annoying to carry out this request, doing it will allow her to feel valued and will improve the quality of our relationship. Therefore, it is worth doing.

The therapist points out the dismissive pattern:

THERAPIST: [To Pete] I don't think you realize it, but you are inadvertently saying to her, "It doesn't bother me if the trash doesn't go out, so it shouldn't bother you." This is how you get in trouble. She feels disregarded and gets upset. She is different from you. The trash doesn't bother you, but she can't ignore it. So here you have an opportunity to say to yourself, "This isn't important to me, but it is to her. I can do this and make her happy."

The therapist's presentation is intended to help Pete understand how he contributes to escalating arguments through his dismissive attitude.

IDENTIFYING THE UNILATERAL ATTEMPT TO PREVAIL PATTERN: "WINNING THE BATTLE BUT LOSING THE WAR"

A spouse may also employ a dismissive attitude in order to do something the partner objects to. The determined spouse does not fully grasp the price that is paid for this type of behavior. He or she may win the battle (get what is wanted) but lose the war (the quality of the relationship).

Consider the following pattern. Over the years, Mary would consult Pete about household purchases and his automatic response was

"No, we don't need that." Eventually, she stopped asking Pete and bought what she wanted without consulting him. He felt disregarded and betrayed, resulting in repetitive arguments.

THERAPIST: [To Mary] I know it is frustrating, but if you buy this sofa without consulting him, he will feel betrayed and will stop speaking to you. How does that help your relationship? You end up with a sofa and an angry, silent husband. Is it worth it? You win the battle but lose the war. I think you are better off trying to tolerate your frustration and discussing it with him.

MARY: But he just says no! He never listens!

THERAPIST: [To Pete] I understand your anger when she goes behind your back. I would like her to discuss this with you, but do you see the bind she is in if your answer is always "no"? If you want her to inform you, you need to be open to what she has to say.

The therapist describes the repetitive pattern: Mary contributes to the problem by going behind Pete's back; Pete contributes to it by not being more open to Mary's wishes. The therapist then moves toward making a coordinated assignment by encouraging Mary to deal with Pete directly and encouraging Pete to be more open and involved.

Weighing What Is Important to Each Partner and Who Should Be Responsive to Whom

When spouses have a clash of needs, it is often difficult to determine which partner should be responsive and which partner should be the recipient of responsiveness. In determining who should be more responsive, the therapist can consider the following: Which spouse's investment in the issue appears to be greater? Which spouse's needs are greatest in the situation? Which spouse's self-esteem is at greatest risk? Which spouse can make accommodations without giving up a core aspect of the self? The overriding principle is that the therapist helps the spouse whose needs are less involved to become more responsive to the spouse whose needs are more involved. Simultaneously the therapist helps the spouse whose needs are more involved to work at *not* sabotaging himself or herself from getting what is wanted by engaging in negative behavior.

Creating an Awareness of the Two Marital Realities: The Task and the Relationship

Many dismissive spouses fail to consider the impact of their behavior on the relationship. The dismissive remark "It will get done; don't worry about it" ignores the reality of the relationship. Despite the dismissive "don't worry about it," the spouse *will* worry about it. The therapist needs to help spouses understand that they are dealing with two simultaneous realities: the immediate task *and* the relationship (i.e., the impact of their behavior on the feelings of the partner).

Consider the following example. Mary and Pete were in a nursery looking at plants. Earlier, Pete had been criticized by his wife and was feeling stupid over the situation. As a result, he was primed to misinterpret other remarks as implying his stupidity. Mary was only marginally aware of this. As they looked at plants together, Pete commented that a particular holly would be a slow grower. Mary believes that she should be able to "tell it like it is." She corrected him, indicating that it was not a slow grower. They began to bicker and their time together was spoiled. As they discuss the incident, the therapist points out that the husband was already smarting over the earlier event and that he was likely to overreact if he felt that he was being corrected.

THERAPIST: [To Mary] Were you aware that he was already feeling embarrassed about the earlier situation?

MARY: Yes, but that plant wasn't a slow grower. I should be able to comment on reality.

THERAPIST: The plant is one reality. There is another reality here. If he feels corrected by you when he is already feeling foolish, he will inevitably get angry. It is predictable. That also is a reality. You have an opportunity to protect the relationship by not correcting him. If you know your spouse well enough, you can predict what will upset him.

MARY: [Looking to shift the responsibility to her husband] If he is that sensitive, then I do have a problem.

THERAPIST: [To Mary] This is a problem! The question is, how do you cope with it? I am suggesting you accept the reality that he is sensitive to being corrected.

Using the Here and Now to Point Out Disregard and Dismissive Attitude

The disregard that spouses complain bitterly about is often present in their interaction during the session. The here and now can be utilized to discuss the destructive pattern.

Pete Looks at the Floor

As Mary discusses an issue that disturbs her, Pete repeatedly looks at the floor. The implicit message is that he is not interested in what she has to say.

THERAPIST: [To Pete] Are you aware that you were looking at the floor when she was talking to you? You looked like you wanted to escape.

THERAPIST: [To Mary] What were you feeling when you were talking to him just now?

The therapist is probing for feelings of disregard.

MARY: Like he just doesn't give a damn about anything that is important to me.

THERAPIST: [To Pete, protecting him by reframing the interaction as unintentional] I don't think you are trying to make her feel bad. [Presenting the pattern] But when you look at the floor, she feels about this big [therapist indicates the size of a thimble]. She feels that you don't care. That is when she gets angry and starts criticizing. This is what we need to work on changing.

The purpose of the here and now intervention is to make a spouse more aware of the impact of a dismissive behavior by identifying it in the session and bringing out the underlying pain the behavior inflicts on the partner.

USING SUPPORT LISTS TO STRUCTURE THE THERAPY AROUND THE ISSUE OF SUPPORT

If the therapist thinks the therapy requires more structure, the sessions can be organized around the issue of support by having the couple compile *support lists*. In introducing support lists, the therapist can say something such as the following:

THERAPIST: To become more supportive you must understand what your partner wants. The list below will help you understand what is important to your partner. Seven areas of marital life are covered: household issues, parenting issues, how you talk to each other, companionship activities, in-laws, your sex life, and the need for alone time. You will be asked to indicate what you want from your partner in each area, how it would help you if your partner supported you in this area, and how it would make you feel if your partner supported you. Creating these lists can help your partner understand what is important to you. Once you have completed the list, you will be asked to rank the items from most important to least important.

Let's consider Mary's and Pete's lists.

Mary's List

Household

- What kind of support do I want from my spouse?
  I want help with cleaning. You say you clean the bathroom, but the tub and toilet are not clean.
- How would this help me?
  It would give me relief. I wouldn't have to worry about doing it.
- How would I feel if my partner did this?
  It would feel like you take me seriously. Also we would be working as a team regarding the housework. That would make me feel better about us.

Parenting

- What kind of support do I want from my spouse?
  I want you to support me by saying "no" when Sammy hasn't done his homework and wants to watch TV.
- How would this help me?
  Sammy doesn't get away with being irresponsible. He needs to be more responsible.

- How would I feel if my partner did this?
  I would feel like I have backup from you and we are on the same team.

How We Talk to Each Other

- What kind of support do I want from my spouse?
  I want to stop arguing all the time. Everything ends up as an argument.
- How would this help me?
  I would be free from the stress of arguing.
- How would I feel if my partner did this?
  Freedom from your put-downs when we argue. They make me feel stupid.

Companionship Activities

- What kind of support do I want from my spouse?
  I would like to go for walks in the evening like we used to.
- How would this help me?
  We would get time together to enjoy the outdoors.
- How would I feel if my partner did this?
  We would get to talk and feel connected.

In-Laws

- What kind of support do I want from my spouse?
  I would like you to defend me when your family starts picking on me.
- How would this help me?
  I won't be uptight around your family.
- How would I feel if my partner did this?
  I would feel that you know how much it upsets me and I would know that you care about me.

Sex Life

- What kind of support do I want from my spouse?
  I wish you would hold me when we are in bed without it being about sex.

- How would this help me?
  It gives me time to relax and feel close. Then I might be interested in sex.
- How would I feel if my partner did this?
  It allows me to feel you take me and my needs seriously.

Alone Time

- What kind of support do I want from my spouse?
  I wish you would watch the kids and let me work in the garden without interruptions.
- How would this help me?
  I can enjoy my gardening and relax.
- How would I feel if my partner did this?
  It shows you understand my need for relief and care enough to make sure I get it.

Pete's List

Household

- What kind of support do I want from my spouse?
  I want you to stop criticizing the way I clean.
- How would this help me?
  It would make it easier for me to get the job done.
- How would I feel if my partner did this?
  Your comments sting. I would be free from feeling incompetent.

Parenting

- What kind of support do I want from my spouse?
  I want you to stop being so harsh with Sammy.
- How would this help me?
  Sammy wouldn't be so rebellious.
- How would I feel if my partner did this?
  I would feel like we are working together.

How We Talk to Each Other

- What kind of support do I want from my spouse?
  Try not to get so angry when we discuss things.

- How would this help me?
  We might actually finish a discussion and settle something.
- How would I feel if my partner did this?
  I would feel better about us.

Companionship

- What kind of support do I want from my spouse?
  I wish we could find time for a weekend away.
- How would this help me?
  We could enjoy ourselves the way we used to.
- How would I feel if my partner did this?
  I would feel that you put me first for once, not fourth on your list of priorities.

In-Laws

- What kind of support do I want from my spouse?
  I don't have a problem with your parents.
- How would this help me?
  It isn't a problem.
- How would I feel if my partner did this?

Sex Life

- What kind of support do I want from my spouse?
  I wish you showed more interest in our sex life.
- How would this help me?
  I could enjoy sex with you.
- How would I feel if my partner did this?
  I would feel like you know how important sex is to me and that you want to please me.

Alone Time

- What kind of support do I want from my spouse?
  I need time to work on my stamp collection without your criticizing me for leaving you alone.

- How would this help me?
  I can enjoy my hobby.
- How would I feel if my partner did this?
  It would feel good knowing you appreciate how important this is to me.

Once Mary and Pete complete their lists, they are asked to rank them from most important to least important.

Mary's Rankings	*Pete's Rankings*
1. Household	1. How we talk to each other
2. Parenting	2. Alone time
3. How we talk to each other	3. Sex life
4. In-laws	4. Parenting
5. Alone time	5. Companionship
6. Sex life	6. Household
7. Companionship	7. In-laws

Pete and Mary are then asked to discuss item one on each list. Mary ranked *household* first. At that moment in their relationship, what Mary wanted most from Pete was his help with the bathroom. Pete was baffled by this. He wondered, "How could this possibly be the most important thing to her?" To him it was superficial and totally unrelated to their relationship. Pete did not understand the degree to which Mary felt that things were inequitable. After discussing it, Pete still did not fully understand. However, since she ranked it first, he concluded it must be important to her. Therefore, he decided he must take it seriously.

Pete ranked *how we talk to each other* first. He wants Mary to try not to get angry when they discuss things. Mary had an easier time grasping why this was important to Pete. She tried not to become defensive during the discussion of this item, but still thought her anger was often justified. Despite this, she too accepted that this was very important to Pete.

Pete and Mary are then given the homework assignment of doing item one on the partner's list. Several weeks should be devoted to executing item one. After progress has been made, they can rerank the items and address next item.

KEEPING THE SUPPORT ISSUE ON THE TABLE AND MONITORING PROGRESS

As the sessions proceed, the therapist will engage in an iterative process. Instances of the support issue will emerge, aspects of the pattern will be described, and assignments will be suggested. The rationale for more supportive behavior will be presented. The therapist will process successes and probe the failures for obstacles. If the therapist is successful, the support issue will lose its salience and other problems in the relationship will become the focus of treatment. The therapist will need to return to the support issue when it is no longer the focus by saying, "How are we doing with regard to support?"

Chapter 6

Dealing with Triangulation Patterns in Subsequent Sessions

When triangular patterns are present, one spouse feels isolated and rejected in the presence of a third party. The rejected spouse will ultimately become angry and attacking, prompting the partner to become defensive. The result is a chronic argument about the third party. Two common triangular patterns are addressed in this chapter: the parenting triangle and the triangle regarding the spouse's work or hobbies. Whatever the source of triangulation, *the goal is to get the couple working together with regard to the triangular threat, thus allowing each to feel supported by the other.* The therapist must present the triangular pattern, bring out painful underlying affect, create assignments that foster detriangulation, probe for obstacles, and follow through.

THE PARENTING TRIANGLE

The parenting triangle often involves arguments over a child's objectionable behavior and the appropriate discipline. The following theme is often present:

1. a child's objectionable behavior;
2. the harsh parent;
3. the overprotective parent; and
4. a parent-child alignment that enmeshes one parent with the child and excludes the other.

One triangular pattern emerges from the wife's perception that the husband is harsh and overbearing. Concerned that the child will be damaged by the husband's harsh treatment, the wife becomes fearful when she sees her husband reprimand the child. As a result, she cannot stay out of the interaction between them, and her interventions undercut the husband's authority. The husband feels demeaned, powerless, and isolated within the family. He becomes overtly angry at his wife and they may argue in front of the child. If this pattern is firmly in place, the child becomes increasingly disrespectful of the harsh father, knowing that the mother is there for backup.

The argument about discipline is often about the relative importance the wife places on maintaining the child's self-esteem versus the husband's emphasis on building the child's independence. Eliciting the perspective of each may reveal the wife's fear that the husband's behavior causes the child to feel rejected and will be damaging to the child's self-esteem. Fearing harm, she undercuts the husband's attempts at discipline. The husband's concern is that the wife is overprotective and indulgent. He fears she will hamper the child's ability to grow up and function autonomously. Although their perspectives can complement one another, instead, they become locked in struggle.

Identifying the Objectionable Behavior

The first step in detriangulation requires that the therapist and couple discuss the child and the behaviors that are a source of contention. The objectionable behavior could be relatively insignificant and involve normal sibling rivalry, avoiding homework, chores, or following rules. Sometimes the objectionable behavior is more serious. The child may be excessively fearful, dependent, or depressed. There may be serious problems with impulse control such as failing classes, stealing money, rebelling against authority, using drugs and alcohol, driving under the influence, or losing jobs. The therapist must seek concrete examples of these behaviors and probe for how the spouses react to the challenge posed by the child or adolescent.

Probing for the Inner Experience of Each

The therapist needs to explore the inner experience of each spouse regarding the child. The therapist needs to probe the wife's fear that the child may be hurt emotionally by the harsh husband. The therapist needs to probe the husband's sense of humiliation when he is treated with disrespect by his wife or child. How do they feel about their other children? What are their expectations regarding their children? Do these expectations seem realistic to the therapist? What are their expectations regarding parenting? During discussion of the troublesome situations, the therapist must acquire information that allows for an assessment of the overall functioning of the child and the functioning of the spouses as parents.

Assessment of the Child (or Adolescent)

In addition to trying to understand the inner experience of each spouse, the therapist is also trying to determine the severity of the behavior in question. Is it within or outside the normal range of misbehavior that all parents must address in the process of child rearing? If the problem behavior is mild and involves not doing chores or not doing homework, the interventions remain within the marital therapy sessions. If the behavior is more severe and involves drugs and/or other illegal activity, referral to other professionals and community agencies is appropriate.

Assessing Parenting

As the therapist probes the inner experience of each spouse, the quality of the parenting is also being evaluated. In doing so, the therapist will consider the following two dimensions.

Dimension One: Do the Parents Love and Adequately Care for the Child?

Do the parents appear to love the child and want what is best for him or her? Parents need to create an environment that allows the child to feel loved and cared for. This is accomplished by being responsive to the child's emotional, physical, and developmental needs. Children who feel loved internalize it as self-acceptance. It becomes an invaluable resource when dealing with life's stresses. However, helping a child develop inner acceptance does not mean overprotecting and insulating the child from realistic demands and criticism. Where do the parents appear to fall on the love-rejection continuum and on the overprotection continuum?

Dimension Two: Do the Parents Define and Adhere to Limits?

Parents need to set and adhere to limits to help the child learn to tolerate frustration and develop self-control. Self-control and the ability to tolerate frustration are essential if the child is to function in the world. In the process of child rearing, this means saying "no" when necessary and arranging negative consequences when the child does not obey clearly stated rules.

The therapist can point out that self-control and self-reliance are crucial if children are to live in a world where they must obey rules, solve problems on their own, and handle situations in which they will be disappointed. A parent cannot help a child develop self-control through indulgence or inconsistency, nor can the parent accomplish it by losing his or her temper, yelling, or engaging in other forms of intimidation.

Where do the parents fall with regard to setting limits and consistently adhering to them? Where do they fall on the anger management continuum?

The therapist will consider these dimensions while discussing problem situations concerning the child. Is the mother saying "yes" when she should be adhering to limits and saying "no"? Is she doing the child's chores, homework, or other tasks that the child needs to do in order to develop self-discipline? Is the father damaging the child's self-esteem, or fostering rebellion, by being harsh, rigid, or excessively demanding? Is either parent's behavior contributing to what becomes a destructive pattern?

Describing the Pattern: Bringing Out Painful Affect and Finding Ways to Reframe the Pattern

Once the therapist understands the experience of each partner and the pattern, he or she will describe the pattern and bring out the painful affect that each spouse experiences within it. Exposing the inner painful affect can be useful in reframing the pattern. The wife's *fear* about her child's well-being must be brought to the surface and examined. If the husband can see that fear for her child prompts her undermining behavior toward him, perhaps he can alter his view of her as controlling or demeaning.

The husband's painful isolation within the family and his sense of *humiliation* when he feels treated with disrespect must be surfaced. If his wife can see that his angry behavior is based on the inner experience of humiliation, perhaps she will see him as less harsh and dictatorial.

Their inner concerns regarding self-esteem and autonomy must also surface. The therapist can point out that although each may see the situation differently, both have the child's best interests in mind. Self-esteem and autonomy are both important and the partners are not as far apart in their hopes for the child as they think. Such reframing may soften their attitudes toward each other.

Reframing the Triangular Situation: What Is Best for Your Child?

In presenting a description of the triangular pattern and looking for ways to bring the couple together, the therapist can reframe the issue in terms of *what is in the best interests of your child?* For example, if the wife cannot say "no" and lets the child win power struggles, the therapist can support the position of the husband:

THERAPIST: I don't think it is good for your child when this happens. It doesn't help him learn how to tolerate frustration and develop self-control.

The therapist may then elaborate on the pattern: The husband sees overindulgence and becomes angry, and the wife defends herself and the child. They argue and remain stuck. The therapist suggests that this pattern must be altered. After processing the material, the wife may agree that for the good of the child she must work harder at saying say "no" and being consistent, thus preventing the child from winning the power struggles.

The therapist may then address the husband and support the position of the wife.

THERAPIST: How is losing your temper and yelling going to help your child? It doesn't help him learn self-control.

The therapist may then point out how his harshness prompts his wife to intervene and become protective. After processing the interaction, the husband may agree that losing his temper is not in the best interest of the child. Agreement in principle is followed by attempts to create coordinated assignments that foster the couple working together as a team with regard to the child, thus detriangulating the situation.

THERAPIST: We need to find ways to get the two of you on the same page, working together and supporting each other.

Typically, the parents have not thought about the child's behavior specifically in terms of self-esteem and autonomy. Nor have they thought clearly about the need for a coordinated response. Introducing the concept of working as a team can be useful. To help the couple work together as a team, the therapist and couple will engage in brainstorming and problem solving regarding the youth's problematic behavior.

WORKING AS A TEAM AND PROBLEM SOLVING

Brainstorming: An Approach to Working As a Team

Agreement in principle must be followed by more specific assignments that allow the couple to work as a team. Defining those specific assignments will *not* be immediately clear. The couple may be angry and seem far apart. The principles that will guide the therapist in bringing them together are those used by any good negotiator.

The first principle is *discerning what is most important to each*. For example, the child's self-esteem is important to the wife and the self-control and respect issues are important to the husband.

The second principle is *the principle of mutual concern*. The discussion must allow each to feel that his or her point of view has been taken seriously by the other during the discussion. In addition, the solution must address the concerns of both parties. If both are comfortable with the proposed solution, then they can work together and support each other.

Finding a mutually agreeable solution requires the use of brainstorming. Brainstorming is a creative process based on thinking "outside the box." The couple is stuck and needs to come up with new ways of responding to the challenging child. Some of the proposed solutions created during brainstorming will be unrealistic. Others will be rejected because one spouse or the other is uncomfortable with them. Some proposed solutions can be reworked and combined until a mutually acceptable approach to the child is developed.

THERAPIST: Let's consider ways you might handle it if your son violates his curfew and is disrespectful. What do you want to do?

With the therapist as mediator, they discuss possibilities. By brainstorming they come up with the following ways of dealing with their adolescent son:

1. Send him to live with a relative
2. Send him to his room
3. Withhold his allowance
4. Ground him
5. Withdraw TV
6. Withdraw music
7. Withdraw the phone
8. Add more chores

If they are to work as a team, each must be comfortable with the proposed response to the objectionable behavior. In this case they agree on withholding the son's allowance and grounding him for one night. They agree to explain this to the child together.

Probing for Obstacles

What might prevent the plan from working? The therapist probes for obstacles. How can we expect the child to behave when he is grounded? Will he become disrespectful? Can the husband remain calm if the son becomes disrespectful? What approach can the therapist employ to help the husband be prepared to stay calm?

The therapist raises the undermining issue. If the son violates his curfew, and the husband follows through with the proposed consequences, can the wife stay out of the husband-son interaction? What might make the wife become concerned about psychological damage to the adolescent that would cause her to intervene? The wife may say that she can refrain from intervening if her husband can remain calm.

When the session draws to an end, the couple may or may not have a plan that will allow them to work together as a team. If they do not, more work can be done at a subsequent session. The therapist reiterates the overall goal, which is to find ways to work together and support each other.

Follow-Up

When assignments have been made, the therapist must follow up. At an appropriate moment in a subsequent session, the therapist will inquire about what transpired. Did they follow through with the agreed-upon approach? If they were successful, the therapist will probe for the internal experience of each and look for any positive consequences. Did they feel that they backed each other up? What was it like to feel supported?

If the assignment failed, the therapist will probe for the obstacles. Was the son disrespectful? What happened when he was? After the therapist probes for the perspective of each spouse, the assignments may be refined. As the sessions continue, other triangular situations regarding parenting will emerge and the therapist will approach each new situation in the manner discussed.

THE WORK OR HOBBY TRIANGLE

The husband's devotion to work or hobbies and his decision to invest long hours in these activities may constitute a source of self-esteem threat for wife. Put simply, the wife's experience is, "You prefer working (hobby) to being with me." A wife's sense of being excluded creates self-esteem threat and self-protective behavior that can wreak havoc in marriage.

The primary intervention when dealing with this type of triangulation is to help the husband develop greater awareness of the importance the wife places on the relationship and the wife's sense of being excluded and feeling insignificant when his attention is elsewhere. With increased awareness, he can often engage in simple behaviors to detriangulate the situation, thereby reducing self-esteem threat for his wife.

Unilateral Assignments

Sometimes the detriangulation suggestions are unilateral. When in potentially triangular situations, spouses can often defuse the situation simply by communicating their awareness of the issue to the partner. Even when engrossed in work, on a business trip, or involved with a recreational activity, the husband can detriangulate the situation by reminding his wife of the importance he places on the relationship. For example, if the husband is going on a business trip, the therapist will encourage the husband to call regularly when he is gone, and encourage the husband to say things such as, "I miss you. What should we do together when I get home? How are things going in my absence?" The husband must then follow through with the promises he has made about what they will do when he returns.

Coordinated Homework Assignments

Sometimes the homework assignments are coordinated. The therapist works with the husband to detriangulate by providing reassurance and with the wife to help her manage her anger more effectively. For example, it will be easier for the husband to call home if he knows that he will not be harassed on the phone. The wife must try to avoid using phone calls to express anger that he is gone or complain that she has all the household responsibilities. Her assignment is to inhibit the angry accusations that cause him to avoid calling her.

A coordinated assignment might also involve helping the wife depersonalize triangular situations. The husband's attention to other activities often implies nothing about how much he loves his wife. She may misinterpret such situations as rejection. The therapist works with the husband to reassure and with the wife to depersonalize.

Probing for Painful Affect and Presenting the Triangular Pattern

When probing for painful affect, the therapist may say to the wife:

THERAPIST: Tell me what it is like for you when he appears preoccupied with his job and doesn't come home until late.

The therapist works to understand the wife's inner experience. As the wife elaborates on her feelings of isolation and rejection, the husband has the opportunity to learn more about his wife's inner life. The therapist might say to the husband:

THERAPIST: Tell me more about what it is like when she attacks you about your job.

The therapist probes the husband's fear that his wife will try to block his career advancement and his sense of betrayal that she would do this. As the therapist probes for painful affect, the wife has the opportunity to learn more about her husband's inner life.

Describing the Pattern

The therapist describes the pattern:

THERAPIST: These fights start when she feels you care more about your work than you do about her. Then she criticizes you about your long hours. Then you become afraid she won't support your career and you argue.

Detriangulation Assignments That Focus on the Pattern

The therapist gives assignments to the husband such as the following:

THERAPIST: If you find ways to reassure her that she is important to you, she may become less angry about your hours.

The therapist gives assignments to the wife such as the following:

THERAPIST: If you can reassure him that you support him in his efforts to succeed at work, he may be less defensive.

Brainstorming and Problem Solving

Brainstorming and problem solving will follow in the manner discussed previously.

THERAPIST: Let's come up with some ideas to accomplish this.

Some of the ideas that may come out of the brainstorming process are the following:

1. The wife can meet the husband for dinner on one of the nights he works late.
2. The husband can call home and check in more often.
3. The wife can try not to complain when he calls.
4. The husband can try harder to listen to his wife when he comes home.
5. The wife can remind herself that he does enjoy her company and wants to be with her.
6. They can plan a weekend away.

Probing for Obstacles and Following Through

The couple decides that items one and three can help them. The wife will meet her husband for dinner at work once a week and she will not complain on the phone. The therapist will probe for obstacles. Will the husband get overwhelmed with work and forget about the dinner? Will the wife be able to edit out her complaining when they talk on the phone? The therapist and couple will consider how they can overcome these obstacles.

As in the earlier example, the therapist will follow up in subsequent sessions, looking for positive consequences if the couple was successful or for obstacles if they did not complete the assignment.

Dealing with Emotional Obstacles to Detriangulating a Hobby Triangle

Reframing the Husband's Fear of Being Restricted

Consider the following example. In the evening, a wife feels threatened by her husband's interest in playing computer games. He appears to prefer this activity to spending time with her. This results in escalating power struggles over how he will spend his time.

The therapist suggests to the husband that he make the first move toward breaking their impasse by assuring his wife that they will spend time together at some point in the evening. His response to the therapist is angry resistance. Why should he be the one to change? He fears losing what little freedom he has. Committing more time to her is a frightening prospect since he thinks her demands are endless. He wants her to get over her insecurity on her own.

The therapist is sympathetic with the husband's desire for free time and reframes the situation in a pragmatic fashion by suggesting that if the husband does constructive behavior A (commit time to her), he may get what he wants (time alone).

THERAPIST: By reassuring your wife that you will spend time with her, you will get your free time. For example, you could say to her, "I am going to be on the computer for an hour; let's watch TV together later." If she believes you, she will be reassured.

HUSBAND: Why can't you work on her irrational jealousy? My computer is not my mistress. That is ridiculous.

THERAPIST: I want to work on that too, but right now, I think we can make faster progress if we work on finding ways to reassure her.

Working to Depersonalize: Example One

In the preceding example, the initial attempt is to encourage the husband to change. This can be followed by attempts to help the wife depersonalize. Some wives often read rejection into situations where it is not present. The husband may value time with his wife even when he is involved in other activities. A reasonable balance of "I" and "we" activities may seem unacceptable to a wife who cannot tolerate her husband's attention being elsewhere. If this is the case, the emphasis will shift to helping the wife depersonalize.

The therapist's message to the wife who reads rejection into situations in which the husband's attention is focused elsewhere is the following:

THERAPIST: Your husband can love you and want to be with you and still want to work late because he wants to be successful. To him they are not connected. He wants both.

Working to Depersonalize: Example Two

A couple is discussing the husband's relationship with his adult daughter. He has spent the last several nights talking to her on the phone. The situation has become triangular for the wife, who feels she has taken a backseat to the daughter. In an attempt to get his attention, she has repeatedly asked him to watch TV with her. He does so for short periods and then calls his daughter. The wife becomes angry and they fight.

THERAPIST: [To the wife] So what was this like for you?
WIFE: At first it was all right. Then it started to bother me.
THERAPIST: How so?
WIFE: He couldn't let go of it. It went on for days. Then we started arguing about it.

The therapist attempts to depersonalize the situation by reframing it in terms of her husband's early experience with his daughter.

THERAPIST: His daughter means a lot to him. He didn't see much of her growing up. Now he has reconnected with her.
WIFE: I can see that.
THERAPIST: I don't think that means he prefers her. She has a certain place in his heart and so do you. When he feels he has both of you, his life is complete. You need to remind yourself that you have a place in his heart she couldn't possibly have.

The therapist attempts to help the wife remind herself of her importance in his life, a belief she quickly loses.

Triangulation Based on Real Avoidance of the Partner

A wife's feelings of rejection may be based in reality. The husband may be staying at work to avoid dealing with his angry wife. A husband's sense of exclusion may be real. His wife may prefer interacting with her children to spending time with him. In such cases, the source of the avoidance must be identified and addressed. Reframing, in these cases, means facing the real rejection and putting the situation in a context that softens the self-esteem threat.

In the following example, the wife's behavior has contributed to her husband refusing to include her in his activities.

Reframing a Husband's Exclusion of His Wife

THERAPIST: [To the wife] I would like him to include you. But the last time he included you, you embarrassed him. If he can be reassured that you won't do that again, maybe he can take the risk and invite you.

Follow-Up

In the previous example, the homework assignment was for the wife to behave more appropriately. As is always the case, the therapist will follow up and process whatever has occurred as a result of the assignment.

Chapter 7

Dealing with Anger Management, Derogation, and Negative Escalation in Subsequent Sessions

Emotionally volatile, impulsive couples are prone to patterns of sudden negative escalation. They are a particular challenge to the therapist. Although the level of therapist activity should be high throughout support-focused marital therapy, the therapist must be prepared to intensify his or her efforts when couples are prone to interrupting, accusing, arguing, and negative escalation. During the derogation-negative escalation pattern, the marital system becomes highly threatening. Spouses must protect their self-esteem by denying wrongdoing and hurling accusations at the partner in what becomes a reciprocal destructive pattern. Although these battles inflict severe damage on the relationship, neither partner is capable of terminating the interaction.

When derogation-negative escalation occurs in the session, a distinct atmosphere develops. As their argument heats up, spouses feel threatened and become more threatening. Attention becomes narrowly focused on the adversary (the partner). Spouses become less aware of the therapist's presence and ignore any attempts at intervention. The therapist will feel increasingly ignored in his or her attempts to get the couple's attention.

The therapist *must* rise to occasion and become more assertive in order to keep the session from spinning out of control. This means throwing oneself into the couple's angry maelstrom and finding ways to halt the destructive interaction and calm the system so that eventually they can *examine* it. If the therapist allows the derogation-negative escalation to continue, the couple will lose faith in the therapist.

The spouses already know how to fight. They have come to therapy for help in getting beyond this pattern.

CALMING THE ANGRY SYSTEM: THE THERAPIST AS GATEKEEPER

As the argument heats up, the therapist can impose structure in the situation by intensifying the gatekeeper role. This means that the spouses must address the therapist, not each other. This can be done informally by simply forcefully intervening and starting a conversation with one or the other. As an alternative, the therapist can impose structure by saying something such as the following:

THERAPIST: Let's call a time out. Nothing productive is going to occur if we continue like this. Let's do this. [Looking at one of them] You talk to me. Then it will be your turn to talk and your spouse can listen.

The therapist becomes the intermediary, receiving messages from one spouse and empathically probing what is heard. The other spouse may not like the self-serving presentation he or she is hearing and will angrily interrupt. The therapist must prevent this and firmly reiterate the format:

THERAPIST: Let's finish hearing from him and then I want to hear your perspective, but please don't interrupt. We can't accomplish anything if there are interruptions.

With the therapist serving as the switchboard, the session moves forward. The goal for the gatekeeper is to take the threat out of the interaction, thereby calming the system.

The Therapist's Tools in the Gatekeeper Role

In the role of gatekeeper with volatile couples, the therapist utilizes many of same tools that have already been described. However, when emotional volatility and negative escalation are present, the therapist must be more vigilant and quicker to intervene to avoid flare-ups.

These tools are

1. empathic probing;
2. serving as an advocate for each spouse;
3. probing for positive intent;
4. correcting misinterpretations;
5. reframing hurtful comments;
6. looking for common ground;
7. preventing the couple from going on tangents; and
8. encouraging the spouses to manage their frustration.

Did You Turn Off the Stove?

Consider the following example. Paul asked his wife, Jane, whether the stove had been turned off. Jane felt Paul was accusing her of being absentminded. Feeling criticized, she counterattacked with, "You are just like your father, always picking." A negative escalation quickly followed both at home and again when they discussed the incident in the session.

Empathic Probing

A spouse's anger will diminish if he or she feels understood. When the marital system is full of acrimony, the therapist must work to understand where each partner is coming from, thereby calming the spouses. In this case, the therapist must work with Paul to understand what prompted the remark. What is this about for him? What thoughts does he typically have when leaving the house? Has there been a history of the stove being left on? Is it about safety, saving money, being orderly?

The therapist must do the same with Jane. What is it about for her? Getting into what the issue means for each spouse is crucial in allowing the spouses to feel understood, thereby calming the system.

Becoming an Advocate for Each Partner

During the negative escalation, each spouse is feeling attacked and will attempt to "monsterize" the other. The therapist must assume that neither are monsters and must look for ways to come to the aid of each spouse and "de-monsterize" each in the eyes of the other.

THERAPIST: I think you are both well intended here, but obviously something goes wrong when you discuss this. Jane hears a put-down and gets angry.

Probing for Positive Intent

A spouse's intent prior to the negative escalation is often benign. In an attempt to de-monsterize the spouse in the eyes of the partner, the therapist will look for positive intent and convey it to the partner. Although Paul frequently does criticize his wife, it appears that this was not his intent in this instance.

THERAPIST: [To Jane] His intent wasn't to put you down. He was just concerned that the stove had been left on. You know he worries about this.

Looking for and Correcting Misinterpretations

The therapist, serving as an advocate, can identify misinterpretations and clarify them, thus attempting to demonsterize each in the eyes of the other.

THERAPIST: [To Jane] I think you are misinterpreting what he said. He said, "Did you leave the stove on?" What you heard was, "There you go again, forgetting things."

Reframing Hurtful Comments

Although initially a spouse's intent may be harmless, when the argument heats up, hurtful comments are made intentionally and the partner's negative interpretation is correct. In serving as an advocate, the therapist can reframe these angry comments. The therapist can acknowledge the hurtful intent, identify the comments as regretful, and point out that a goal of therapy is to eliminate them.

The therapist can then attempt to get behind the "zingers" each has hurled at the other and reinterpret them as self-protective. In the previous example, Jane overreacted to her husband's question about the stove. Angrily, she counterattacked with, "Why are you always checking up on me? You are not my father." Paul, feeling attacked, responded with the following self-protective put-down: "Someone has to. You are irresponsible."

THERAPIST: [To Jane] Saying that you are irresponsible was a put-down. He shouldn't have said it. I think he felt attacked and lost control.

Functioning As a Mediator and Looking for Common Ground

Usually, much common agreement between spouses is obscured by their battle. The therapist, functioning as a mediator, can look for areas of common agreement. As with any good negotiator, the therapist must latch on to these aspects of the interaction and put them on the table for discussion. Finding common ground allows the couple to feel closer and produces a calming effect:

THERAPIST: You both agree you don't want the stove left on. Actually, you agree on many things, but the accusations and misinterpretations get in the way.

Preventing Spouses from Going on Tangents

Volatile couples are notorious for "throwing in everything but the kitchen sink" as they try to score points at the expense of their spouses. In the role of gatekeeper, the therapist must keep the couple on task:

THERAPIST: It is not going to be helpful to talk about fathers. I would like to return to the stove issue.

Encouraging the Spouses to Stay Engaged Despite Frustration

The therapist can point out the role frustration plays in negative escalation. Each spouse feels misunderstood and becomes frustrated. The therapist can attempt to structure the interaction around the issue of frustration:

THERAPIST: I want the two of you to try to discuss this without giving in to your frustration and making an angry remark. If you think your frustration is going to get the best of you, call a time-out.

Calming a Derogatory System with Empathic Probing: "I Am Not Selfish; You Are"

Jane and Paul have been fighting all week after she called him "selfish." The incident involved Paul making vague references to taking the kids to the pool and then not following through with it. Jane's accusation that he was selfish infuriated Paul. At some level he knows he was guilty, but within their threatening marital system it is not safe for him to acknowledge his mistake. He resents being called selfish when he works hard to support his family. Instead of being appreciated for his efforts, he is accused of selfishness.

During the session they begin to "throw in everything but the kitchen sink" as their accusations and counter-accusations escalate. The therapist begins to calm the system by focusing on Jane and engaging in empathic probing. What is this about for Jane? The therapist wants to walk around in her experience.

THERAPIST: [Raising her voice in order to be heard and addressing the wife] Tell me more about what it was that bothered you.

JANE: The kids need to have something to do. I was busy that day. It was his responsibility to take care of them and interact with them, not ignore them.

THERAPIST: So you were concerned about the kids were being ignored.

JANE: I thought he was being thoughtless.

The therapist wants to serve as gatekeeper and convey the wife's perspective to the husband, stripped of its angry, attacking quality.

THERAPIST: [To Paul] She is saying that what bothered her was that you were not thinking about what the kids needed and you were not interacting with them.

PAUL: I thought the kids were fine. They were watching T.V.

THERAPIST: But can you see where she might be concerned that you were ignoring them?

The therapist conveys the wife's perspective to the husband. If the husband can acknowledge an aspect of her experience, the marital system will become calmer.

PAUL: [Reluctantly] I can see that.
THERAPIST: Do you think they were feeling ignored?
PAUL: I didn't think so. They seemed fine.
THERAPIST: So from your perspective, everything was fine.

As the therapist probes, the husband elaborates on his perspective and the therapist conveys his perspective to Jane. The therapist has been able to serve as an advocate for both spouses and has clarified some of the underlying concerns. By dealing empathically with each, serving as the gatekeeper, and conveying perspectives, the therapist has helped to calm the system.

More on Correcting Misinterpretations to Calm the System

Consider the therapist's role in correcting misinterpretations in the following example. A flare-up culminates with a husband angrily shouting at his wife and an ensuing period of silent hostility. Processing the interaction revealed that the problem began when the husband was attempting to fix the lawn mower. He was frequently on the defensive regarding his mechanical abilities. On this occasion the wife could see that his hands were encumbered and tried to help. He interpreted her behavior as implying that he was doing something wrong. Actually, she had been appreciative of his efforts; however, she could see his hands were full and she wanted to help.

THERAPIST: [To the husband] It sounds as if she thought you were doing fine. She was just trying to help. I think you misinterpreted the situation.

If the husband can interpret his wife's intent in a more benign light, the system will become calmer.

Consider correcting a misinterpretation of intent in the following situation. Paul has repeatedly told Jane to stay out of his sister's marital problems. As he addresses her in the session, his tone is frustrated and accusatory. Jane gets defensive and angry. They argue. She accuses him of trying to control and demean her. This intensifies his anger. They remain stuck in their hostile positions. The wife's position is: You are trying to control and demean me. The husband's position is: You are being willful.

The therapist will want to explore the situation, hoping to understand it and calm the system. Empathic probing with each reveals the following:

- What was Jane's intent? What did she want?
  She was trying to help the sister by asking questions.
- What was Paul's intent? What did he want?
  He was trying to help his sister by protecting her privacy.
- What was Jane's inner experience of her husband?
  She experienced the husband as controlling and demeaning toward her.
- What was Paul's inner experience of his wife?
  He experienced his wife as intrusive and willful toward him. She would not listen to him.

Correcting Jane's Misinterpretation

Once the therapist understands the situation, he or she attempts to present the husband's intent in a more benign light, thereby calming the system.

THERAPIST: [To Jane] You feel he is trying to control you, but what I hear is different. He didn't handle it well because he got frustrated, but his motive was to protect his sister, not control you.

TEACHING THE COUPLE TO AVOID NEGATIVE ESCALATION

Once the system has been calmed, the therapist can begin to analyze the steps in their "dance" so that they can anticipate and avoid the destructive sequence. The therapist may inquire about the moments, hours, or days prior to a negative escalation to determine the slights or misinterpretations that may have led to it. As the therapist and couple discuss the steps in their dance, the therapist will elicit the subjective experience of each and surface how each experienced the interaction in terms of self-esteem threat and subsequent self-esteem protection.

THERAPIST: So when she said X, you felt put down and hurt. Then you retaliated by saying Y. Then she felt put down and did Z.

By broadening the context to include earlier precipitating events, spouses can escape from their own egocentric perspectives as victims in the interaction. The problem is reframed as broader than either of them; it becomes their marital system. Each spouse is encouraged to take responsibility for his or her own steps in their dance that contributed to the negative escalation:

THERAPIST: I know you were hurt by his remark B. I think he said B because he was wounded by your remark A.

Using Problem Solving to Avoid Negative Escalation: How Could They Have Handled It Differently?

After the pattern has been examined, the therapist can turn to problem solving and ask the question, "How might you have handled it differently?" The therapist wants to consider what each spouse might have said or done differently that might have avoided the negative escalation. Since spouses are defensive about their own contributions to the negative escalation, the therapist must proceed with care.

THERAPIST: [To Jane] So you were angry when you heard that Paul ignored the kids. I wonder how you might have brought this up to him without calling him "selfish."
JANE: I don't know. It still makes me angry.
THERAPIST: Perhaps you could have made it a question, "Why didn't you take them to the pool? I don't understand."

The therapist and Jane continue to discuss how she might have handled the situation differently.

FRAMING THE ISSUE AS ANGER MANAGEMENT

Negative escalation is fueled by the spouses' difficulties with anger management. Anger management is a pervasive problem in distressed marriages. Many spouses have histories of inappropriate anger expression that predate the marriage. For others, their ability to control their anger has been worn away by marital conflict. In addition to raised voices and derogatory remarks, they provoke each other by slamming doors, going off in a huff, refusing to communicate, retrieving gifts, canceling accounts, retracting promises, giving the other the silent treatment, provoking jealousy, etc. When the system has been calmed, the negative escalation can be framed as one of inappropriate anger management.

The unit of analysis switches from the spouses' inner experiences to the impulsive and inappropriate ways they handle their anger when it is triggered. The therapist labels the angry and impulsive behavior as "inappropriate anger management," and suggests that the spouses must find less damaging ways to cope in frustrating situations.

FRAMING INAPPROPRIATE ANGER MANAGEMENT AS A FUNCTION OF MARITAL DETERIORATION

One approach is to frame a spouse's lack of control as the result of marital deterioration. This reframing may reduce defensiveness.

THERAPIST: [To Jane] The years of feeling disregarded have taken their toll on you. Your fuse has become shorter. Your voice sounds angry and impatient. Unfortunately, this happens when marriages deteriorate.

The "No Excuse for Loss of Control" Reframe

Since blame-oriented spouses will not want to accept responsibility for their own loss of control, identifying the issue as inappropriate anger management often requires therapist confrontation. The therapist must become an advocate for what is universally acceptable behavior and must convey that what the spouse is doing is unacceptable.

The therapist can minimize the threat by softening the confrontation with an empathic response, for example, "I know you are feeling rejected. . . ." However, the therapist must then focus on the unacceptable behavior. Although the spouse will recognize the wisdom in what the therapist is saying and will respect the therapist for saying it, he or she will not be pleased with the message.

When the anger is explosive, the model that the therapist adopts is similar to that used when dealing with physical abuse. When dealing with physical abuse, the therapist's approach is the following:

THERAPIST: Regardless of the provocation, there is no excuse for violent behavior. The party feeling provoked must exert sufficient self-control to inhibit the violent act. Violence is unacceptable regardless of the level of provocation.

Although the situations the therapist is dealing with usually do not involve physical violence, the approach is the same. When confronting spouses with their difficulties with anger management, the therapist adopts the following position:

THERAPIST: I know you are feeling hurt. Regardless of what your spouse has said or done, you should have sufficient impulse control to handle your anger more effectively. Saying or doing X, Y, or Z is inappropriate and makes your situation worse. We must work to develop other ways to handle situations in which you become angry.

Door Slamming and Plate Throwing

Jane and Paul have not spoken to each other for days. The problem began after their return from the store. Soon after they arrived home, a triangular issue arose. Paul overreacted, stormed out of the house, and slammed the door behind him, breaking the hinge. Negative escalation ensued, culminating with Jane following Paul out of the house and throwing a plate at him.

In the session each blames the other for the escalation. The therapist becomes confrontive, focusing on their difficulties with anger management.

THERAPIST: [To Paul] You feel hurt, get angry at her, storm out of the house, and slam the door. I guess you wanted to show how much she had hurt you. But when you slam the door, you are out of control. You need to find another way to deal with your anger in that situation.

THERAPIST: [To Jane] He won't apologize for his behavior. You feel hurt, and throw a plate in response. That is an unacceptable way to express your anger.

Problem Solving: How Else Could You Have Handled It?

The therapist and couple then consider *how else* they might have handled the situation.

THERAPIST: [To Paul] Slamming the door says, "I am really upset about this." How else could you have gotten that message across?

Paul and the therapist discuss what he might have said to Jane as an alternative to door slamming.

THERAPIST: [To Jane] He must have hurt you badly for you to behave like that. How else do you think you could have handled that?

Jane and the therapist discuss what she might have said to Paul as an alternative to plate throwing.

Using the Here and Now to Point Out Derogation

When spouses direct put-downs to each other in the session, the therapist can use the immediate moment to point out how the destructive pattern begins. This is also an opportunity to bring out the painful emotion that the partner experiences when he or she is on the receiving end of the derogatory remark. Jane and Paul are discussing driving:

PAUL: [The husband is tense and his voice rises.] Look, you are an idiot when it comes to directions!

THERAPIST: [To Paul] These are the kinds of comments that you pay for later. You become derogatory. Then she becomes hostile and you wonder why.

THERAPIST: [To Jane] What were you experiencing as he was talking?

JANE: Like I was a stupid child.

In the heat of battle, the negative impact of the husband's derogatory remark is not apparent to him. By eliciting the wife's painful affect, the impact of derogatory behavior becomes more apparent. In spite of their flare-ups, the husband does not want to be hurtful to his wife.

Assigning Tasks

Once spouses can agree that they want to avoid the negative escalation pattern, they can accept the assignment of monitoring their behavior and trying to cope with their anger differently. The assignments can be specific, e.g., keep a log of the times you felt angry and write down how you tried to cope. The assignments can also be more general, e.g., keep a mental note of angry moments and be prepared to discuss them in the therapy session.

DEALING WITH THE EMOTIONAL OBSTACLES TO ANGER MANAGEMENT AND THE INHIBITION OF CRITICISM

When making assignments, the therapist must be prepared to deal with obstacles and resistance. Consider how the therapist deals with the following obstacles.

Dealing with Paul's Belief That Jane Should Change

Paul's goal for therapy is that Jane be less angry at him. The therapist has linked Jane's constant anger to his tendency to belittle her and has suggested that Paul work on inhibiting his criticism. Paul resists:

PAUL: If she would stop doing these things then I wouldn't have to criticize.
THERAPIST: We can work with her on that. However, if you want her to be less angry, the most effective way to accomplish that is to work on inhibiting your criticisms.

Reframing Angry Outbursts As an Attempt to Be Heard

One nonthreatening way of helping a spouse inhibit angry criticism is to describe the raised voice and the angry outburst as an attempt to be heard. Using this approach, the therapist might reframe the outburst as based on a spouse's fear that if he or she is not loud and angry enough, he or she will not be heard. The therapist must point out the futility of the attempt, since it elicits only defensiveness in the partner:

THERAPIST: [To Jane] When you get frustrated, you begin to raise your voice, as if he will understand if you say it louder. That won't work. He stops listening. How can I help you become more patient?

Reframing the Belief That Angry Criticism Is Justified

Spouses derive a variety of advantages from angry criticism. For some there is a sense of moral superiority. For example, many wives experience moral outrage at their husband's nonsupportive behavior. Therefore they believe their angry criticism is justified. For some, criticizing a spouse creates a sense of intellectual superiority or enhanced competence. The derogatory behavior yields a momentary self-esteem boost, i.e., I am better than you in the arena in which I criticize you. For others, the criticism is defensive and temporarily wards off self-esteem threat.

Most spouses are unaware of the secondary gain that their criticism yields. *The therapist will* not *try to create an awareness of the payoff derived from angry criticism.* Attempts to do so usually provoke defensiveness and confusion. Instead, more pragmatic types of reframings are utilized.

When addressing the issue, the therapist will first take the empathic position and validate the spouse's sense of moral outrage. The therapist may say, "Yes, the partner is indeed engaging in bad behavior. I understand where your anger is coming from." However, the therapist must then point out the futility of lashing out with criticism. For example, the therapist might say:

THERAPIST: [To Jane] I don't blame you for feeling angry. I would like to see him become more supportive. However, when you attack him, he shuts down and doesn't hear you. People who are under attack freeze and become self-protective. Then nothing changes. Let's think about how else to get your message across.

Reframing the Belief That the Partner Is Oversensitive and Should Change

Spouses may resist inhibiting their critical remarks based on the assumption that the partner is oversensitive and should get over this sensitivity. They may even evoke the partner's low self-esteem as an excuse to justify their behavior, e.g., my criticism is normal; his reaction is abnormal and should change. They may believe that they have no responsibility for their partner's self-esteem problem.

A basic assumption of support-focused marital therapy is that spouses are responsible for the feelings of their partners. The therapist may begin to address this by universalizing the criticism experience, i.e., no one likes to be criticized; it is unpleasant for everyone.

The therapist might go on to suggest that the partner may indeed be particularly sensitive to criticism; however, this is unlikely to change. Pragmatically, it might be suggested that more progress can be made by inhibiting critical remarks than by trying to toughen up the partner.

Consider the following example. The therapist has encouraged Jane to be less critical and has pointed out how her criticism of Paul results in the arguments they both dread. Jane replies that her criticisms should "roll off his back." The therapist replies:

THERAPIST: I wish they would roll off his back. I am sure he does too, but that is unlikely to happen. I think you are better off accepting him the way he is and figuring out how to cope differently.

Describing the Marital System As the Obstacle

If the marital system is self-esteem threatening, the spouse's derogatory behavior is often self-protective. The obstacle to reducing angry criticism is the threatening marital system itself. The therapist can describe the pattern of derogation and negative escalation and suggest that although each partner is a victim of it, each has a role in changing it.

THERAPIST: Both of you say hurtful things when your arguments heat up. I don't think either of you wants to be doing this. You are just protecting yourselves in this threatening environment. This reciprocal pattern has gotten out of control. We need to change it.

Depersonalizing Put-Downs

Spouses often accept their partners' put-downs as valid and end up feeling unworthy or incompetent. When attempting to depersonalize a put-down, the therapist helps the spouse who is being criticized to find ways to alter his or her inner dialogue in a way that reduces the negative impact of the remark:

THERAPIST: You are okay. He may put you down, but that does not make you incompetent. The problem is his need to blame others, not anything you have done.

Consider the following example. Jane became furious after Paul accused her of misplacing their cell phone. Although she knew she was innocent, she still bought into his criticism and experienced herself as a "bad" person.

Paul was aware of his tendency to impulsively blame others and had discussed it with the therapist earlier. In this instance, the therapist reminds Jane that Paul has been working to avoid blaming others; however, in this case he slipped. The therapist then attempts to help Jane depersonalize the accusation.

THERAPIST: I want you to write this down. "I have done nothing wrong. He has a problem with blaming others." [Jane writes it down.]

THERAPIST: Now read it to yourself. [Jane reads it.] What do you feel as you read it?

JANE: I feel better.

THERAPIST: Can you keep that in your purse and refer to it when you start to get angry at him?

JANE: I will try.

THERAPIST: Good. Next time let's see if it helped.

Paul squirmed uncomfortably when the therapist described him as having a problem with blaming others. However, he trusted the therapist and hoped that this intervention might free him from his wife's angry explosions.

Following Up

The therapist will inquire throughout the sessions about any changes in the level of anger and criticism in the relationship. The therapist will inquire, "What happened last week with regard to criticism?"

Probing for Inhibition of Angry Criticism: Making Covert Behavior Overt

Carrying through with an anger assignment means engaging in self-control and *not* doing something. When a spouse is successful in inhibiting angry criticism, the occasion may go unnoticed by the partner, who has no knowledge of what is occurring within the spouse. In their daily lives it is unlikely (and unwise) for the spouse to say, "I just got angry but withheld a critical remark." Although counterproductive at home, it is useful to discuss such instances in a therapy session. The therapist must probe to make such private efforts at inhibition overt. The therapist will say to a spouse:

THERAPIST: Have you been trying to handle your anger differently this past week?

Such probing may allow the spouse to discuss successful, but private, efforts to inhibit angry behavior during the preceding week. Only by making these successful covert efforts overt is evidence available to the partner that the spouse is working to improve the relationship. Processing the specific successes and failures in managing anger is the therapist's ongoing task.

Chapter 8

Dealing with Communication Avoidance in Subsequent Sessions

WHAT IS DIRECT COMMUNICATION?

Direct communication occurs when spouses respond in the immediacy of the moment with what is on their minds. If their partners have done something that is bothering them, they say so. If they have a desire, they express it. If they need information, they ask the partners questions. If they have made plans, they tell the partner about them.

Direct communication requires spontaneity. It also requires a belief that it is safe to say what is on one's mind. Spouses who communicate directly expect that their partners' response will be accepting. Or if they expect that their partners' response will be anger or disapproval, they believe that they can tolerate it.

INDIRECT COMMUNICATION AND CONFLICT AVOIDANCE

Indirect communication is often fear based and occurs when spouses do not feel safe to say what they are thinking. Spouses who have trouble communicating directly do not believe it is safe to speak out spontaneously. Fear that the partner will become controlling or angry makes it unsafe. Anger is a particularly difficult emotion for spouses who have difficulty with direct communication. Although no one likes to deal with an angry partner, for a conflict-avoidant spouse the partner's anger is terrifying. However, by not speaking out and getting one's needs met, the silent spouse's resentment grows. The accumulated resentment results in sullen withdrawal or passive aggressiveness that increases the insecurity and loneliness of both spouses.

If there appears to be a lack of direct communication about expressing one's needs, the therapist must work to increase spontaneity and direct communication. Unlike the lack of support pattern, where a partner disregards a spouse's expressed needs, here disregard comes about because the partner is unaware of just what the spouse's needs are.

DESCRIBING THE COMMUNICATION AVOIDANCE PATTERN

Why Didn't You Tell Me? Working with Maureen and Max

Maureen and Max are living together and are considering marriage. Both are secretive and conflict avoidant. They live in Max's apartment and Max does little to contribute to their daily lives by cooking or helping with her kids. Maureen is resentful about this. Both appear to fear being controlled by the other. In addition, Max goes off for hours without telling Maureen where he is. Maureen is suspicious that he is with other women when he disappears.

Maureen alludes to these issues from time to time but cannot keep them on the table for discussion. Her resentment builds and is expressed in passive-aggressive behavior. She recently joined a new church without telling Max. He found out when the minister called, and he felt embarrassed about not being informed. He wants more open communication with Maureen but appears to disregard her vaguely expressed complaints, thus contributing to her distrust and silence.

Probing for the Inner Experience of Each

The therapist works with Maureen to understand her inner experience. This is difficult as she tends to be reserved. With empathic probing, Maureen reveals her painful experience of distrust. She says that she felt controlled in other relationships and she is fearful of finding herself in that painful position again. Now, she lurches between dependence and independence. She wants to be open with Max, but then pulls back, fearing he will attempt to control her and believing that she must rely only on herself. The therapist wonders how her husband is reacting to her painful self-disclosure. Does he understand the depth of her fear? Does he understand how his behavior triggers it? Later the therapist will present the pattern and try to help Max see the connection.

The therapist works with Max to understand his inner experience. He appears cut off from his inner life and cannot share a great deal. There will be no painful self-disclosures from him. The therapist's impression is that Max is highly task oriented and not accustomed to thinking about relationships. However, he clearly wants a better relationship with Maureen. He tells Maureen that there are no other women in his life. The therapist probes, asking about the situations that have created distrust. The therapist listens and senses that Max wants his freedom of movement but is not involved with other women.

The therapist conveys Maureen's perspective to Max regarding feeling controlled. The therapist says to Max, "She feels if she tells you what she wants you will oppose it. What is your sense of this?" Max says he understands, but then defends himself.

Describing the Pattern and Working on Maureen's Contribution to It

The therapist describes the pattern of communication avoidance and how it leads to resentment and secretive behavior.

THERAPIST: [To Maureen] He did nothing when you mentioned the meals and the kids, so you dropped it and your resentment built. Then you thought to yourself, "He doesn't want to help, I am in this alone, I'll do my own thing." Then he was blindsided by the church situation and felt excluded. Can you see how he would feel excluded when you don't tell him about these things?

MAUREEN: I know you are right. I am just afraid to.

THERAPIST: Afraid? How so?

MAUREEN: Maybe I am afraid that if I tell him, he will take control. That is what happened in my other relationships.

The therapist and Maureen discuss her feelings of being controlled. Hopefully, Max is absorbing some of what is discussed. Her fear of being controlled and exploited is powerful. The therapist attempts to connect empathically with her fear, then moves beyond empathy and emphasizes the need to take the risk and communicate.

THERAPIST: I know you are afraid of losing control, but I think it is important to take the risk and tell him what you want. Otherwise, your resentment will grow. If you feel you are losing control, bring it up in here so we can prevent it.

The therapist encourages risk taking, in the form of more open communication, and suggests using the sessions as a backup so Maureen will not lose control.

Describing the Pattern and Working with Max's Contribution to It

THERAPIST: [To Max] She feels that you are not helping with the kids. So she gets resentful and then won't communicate. Can you see how this makes her feel resentful?

The therapist focuses on how Max contributes to Maureen's resentment. The therapist points out how his behavior blocks him from getting what he wants, which is more open communication from Maureen.

THERAPIST: If you want her to be more open, you need to help her with her resentment. When she feels resentful, she clams up.

Assignments

The therapist's initial suggestions are broad. Maureen should try and discuss what was on her mind with Max. Max was encouraged to do the same. He was also given the more specific assignment of reassuring Maureen by calling her more often and informing her of his whereabouts.

The therapist also suggested they set aside a time each day for discussion of the events of their respective days. The therapist doubted they would actually do it; however, the assignment reinforces the message: discuss issues more openly and directly.

DEALING WITH OBSTACLES TO DIRECT COMMUNICATION

The obstacles to more direct communication are often fear based. Fear of the partner's anger, fear of an argument, and fear of losing control often block attempts at more direct communication.

Reframing Fear of the Partner's Anger: The "Pay Me Now or Pay Me Later" Metaphor

Fear of the partner's anger can be reframed by discussing the negative consequences of communication avoidance. One approach is to use the "pay me now or pay me later" metaphor.

THERAPIST: You can pay twenty dollars for an oil change now or one thousand dollars for a new engine later. The momentary discomfort of speaking up is less painful than the long-term resentment that builds when you keep quiet.

The message the therapist wants to convey is that by avoiding the short-term discomfort of possible partner anger, the spouse pays a greater price later—that is, intense resentment and a deteriorating marriage.

Depersonalizing the Partner's Anger

Attempting to depersonalize the partner's anger is also useful in encouraging more direct communication. For example, the therapist may say the following:

THERAPIST: If your partner gets angry, it does not mean that you have done something wrong. By speaking up and avoiding resentment you are protecting the long-term health of your relationship. You need to say to yourself, "I am speaking up for the good of the relationship. If my partner gets angry, I have done nothing wrong."

Dealing with Fear of Loss of Control Through Coordinated Assignments

Some spouses fear that if they are open about what they want, they will *not* get it. The therapist can use coordinated homework assignments to deal with this fear.

If Maureen is afraid to tell Max about the church because she expects him to oppose it, then the therapist can work with Max to minimize this possibility by encouraging Max to be more accepting when Maureen brings it up. If he can do so, perhaps Maureen can take the risk and tell him.

If Max is reluctant to tell Maureen that he is having drinks with friends, expecting her to become suspicious and angry, then the therapist will work with Maureen to be more accepting when he calls. If she can do so, perhaps Max can take the risk and call her.

The therapist can also work on giving Max and Maureen the coping skills they need to discuss issues directly. Does Max know how to reassure Maureen on the phone? The therapist can help Max come up with the words he needs when talking to Maureen. He can help Maureen do the same.

Dealing with Conflict Avoidance by Problem Solving Within the Session

Conflict-avoidant spouses evade what appear to be trivial issues. When the therapist encourages them to discuss a seemingly simple issue at home, they procrastinate. The therapist can use the here and now of the session to confront these avoided topics. For example, if they have avoided discussing the kids and meals, they can discuss them in the session.

THERAPIST: Let's talk about meals. How do you want to divide them up?

If the therapist puts the issue on the table for discussion, the couple will reluctantly follow and begin a discussion.

Using the Here and Now of the Session to Encourage Direct Communication

Saying What He Thinks and Feels

Let us consider with another couple an example of a way in which the therapist can use the here and now of the session to encourage direct communication. Clarice has complained to the therapist about her husband Alvin's long periods of silence. At such moments she feels isolated and insecure. Alvin's silence often occurs when he broods about an experienced slight. His aversion to expressing himself is so intense that on many occasions he is unaware of having any feelings at all.

When Clarice tries to pull feelings out of him, he retreats still further into himself. During the sessions, Alvin has begun to understand more clearly how his resentment leads him to punish his wife with silence. The therapist observes Alvin brooding and comments on it.

THERAPIST: [To Alvin] You seem quiet. Is something on your mind?
ALVIN: No.
THERAPIST: I am reluctant to pursue this because you withdraw if someone tries to pull feelings out of you, but can you identify anything that is bugging you?
ALVIN: [Reluctantly] There was one thing. When I took the kids to soccer practice this morning, I realized that I was annoyed. It wasn't my turn to take them, but here I was, doing it again.
THERAPIST: That is the type of thing you resent. You felt taken advantage of.
THERAPIST: [To Clarice] Did you know this?
CLARICE: No, this is the first I have heard of it.
THERAPIST: [To Alvin] Can you tell her how you feel about this?

The therapist has used the here and now to comment on Alvin's withdrawn state. Alvin, with some trepidation, is able to express his resentment.

Following Up with Assignments

The therapist must keep the communication avoidance issue on the table by saying things such as the following:

THERAPIST: How did it go last week with regard to discussing issues directly?
How is it going with regard to calling home?
How is it going with regard to avoiding resentment?
How is it going with regard to chores?
Did you discuss the meals?

The therapist follows up by processing successes in direct communication and looking for payoffs, and also by processing failures in direct communication and probing for obstacles. Patience and perseverance are crucial. When avoidance of direct communication is based on fear, progress is often slow and difficult.

Chapter 9

Encouraging Companionship, Affection, and Sexual Intimacy in Subsequent Sessions

Support, detriangulation, anger management, and communication avoidance interventions are designed to take anger out of the marital system. One can think of these interventions as bringing the relationship from negative to neutral. However, most couples want more than the absence of anger and a neutral relationship. They want to be friends and lovers. They want affection and intimacy. This is not possible when the marital system is threatening. However, even when threat has been reduced somewhat by the interventions described previously, companionship and intimacy do not necessarily follow. The spouse's self-protective barriers often remain in place.

The therapist must focus on activities that will lower the self-protective barriers. If the couple can engage in pleasurable companionship and sexual activities, the need for self-protection will be diminished and the barriers will be lowered. The therapist must try to move the couple toward such experiences.

USING THE HERE AND NOW TO ENACT AFFECTIONATE BEHAVIOR

Often, the absence of affection is obvious in the session. During a session a partner may remain "frozen" and unable to respond to the spouse's obvious pain with a genuinely caring response. The therapist can comment on the absence of a caring or affectionate response and point out how this has created problems in their relationship.

The therapist must engage in empathic probing with the frozen spouse to attempt to understand the emotional obstacle that blocks a more caring response. Is the frozen spouse angry, fearful, or inhibited? Consider the following example. Joan and Steve are wary of each other. Each has been repeatedly hurt by the other, and they have begun to live parallel lives.

Dealing with Steve's Frozen Style

During a session Joan expresses her dismay that Steve cannot reach out and comfort her. Steve reacts by appearing rigid and impassive.

Empathic Probing to Understand Steve's Inner Experience

The therapist observes:

THERAPIST: I think your wife is in pain and it seems difficult for you to help her. I wonder what the obstacles are that make this so difficult.

Steve shrugs and says he does not know. Joan says she thinks he is trying to punish her for a her disregard of him in the past. The therapist asks Steve about this. As the therapist probes his feelings, it is clear that Steve is still angry at his wife.

THERAPIST: You are stuck right now. Do you want to move beyond this?

The husband acknowledges that he does; however, he can say no more at the moment. An issue has been identified, and a goal has been defined that they will return to.

Using Enactment to Help Joan Hear Caring

Later, following other interventions, Steve has become more openly affectionate. When he does so during the session, Joan, despite her expressed desire for affection, remains frozen.

Empathic Probing to Understand Joan's Inner Experience

THERAPIST: [To Joan] What did you experience when he reached out to you just then?

JOAN: I am afraid to believe it. I can't trust him.

The therapist probes to understand Joan's inner experience. She is ambivalent about feeling close to Steve. The therapist uses the here and now of the session to help her take the risk and allow Steve to get close.

THERAPIST: [To Steve] Tell her again why you care.

STEVE: [With some intensity] You mean everything to me. I do care about you!

The therapist continues to encourage enactment of caring during the session to help overcome the spouse's distrust. The following kinds of statements may prompt caring responses:

THERAPIST: Can you tell her what it is you appreciate about her?
THERAPIST: Tell him what it was about him that you found appealing.
THERAPIST: I sense you do care for her. Can you tell her that?

If the therapist senses genuine caring, the session can be used to have spouses enact it. Such moments can be powerful and can result in the lowering of self-protective barriers. The therapist will also attempt to lower the barriers by encouraging companionship and sexual activities.

ENCOURAGING COMPANIONSHIP

Understanding Each Spouse's Desire for Companionship

The therapist begins to encourage Steve and Joan to engage in companionship activities, probing to determine what each wants in the way of companionship. Asking spouses what they have enjoyed doing together usually reveals activities such as going for walks; going to movies or out to dinner; dancing; socializing with friends; visiting relatives; shopping together; taking the kids to a park, museum, or sports event; working together on a household project, watching TV; snuggling; discussing the events of the day and gossiping about people they both know.

Wives are often more articulate about their companionship expectations. They want such activities to involve verbal interaction and the sharing of experiences. To them, engaging in companionship activities is a form of relationship building, a concept that may be unfamiliar to many of their more autonomous husbands. Although men may be less articulate about their companionship expectations, they clearly want the activity to involve a happy, affectionate, and interested partner.

Encouraging Companionship: Homework Assignments

After discussions of what they have done together in the past and might want to do together now, the therapist might suggest that they take a walk together or watch TV together. Potential obstacles need to be discussed. What might prevent this from occurring?

Anticipating Obstacles

The therapist will wonder aloud, What might cause them to avoid the assignment or have it go badly? Will they argue about what to watch or when to leave for their walk? Will they dawdle about getting started, resulting in one feeling that the other is not interested? During the activity will they argue and spoil their time together? If the therapist and the couple can anticipate potential problems, the couple can avoid them.

Processing Attempts at Companionship: Describing the Pattern and Following Up

At the next session the therapist will inquire about what happened. Did they do the assignment? If so, what was it like? Did it go well or badly? If it went well, the therapist will want to understand the experience of each.

Probing for Positive Consequences If the Assignment Went Well

If the assignment went well, the therapist will probe for positive consequences. What was enjoyable about it? Did they feel closer to each other? Did it improve the quality of their relationship that day?

Probing for Obstacles If the Assignment Was Avoided or Went Badly

Initially, the assignment may be avoided. If they did not do it, assume they are still wary of each other and fear putting themselves in a vulnerable position where they could be rejected. Spouses will not express this directly; however, their self-protection is obvious in their behavior. They could not find the time, had to work late, were distracted by the kids, could not find a baby-sitter, were exhausted, etc.

The therapist will not necessarily comment on their self-protective avoidance of each other. Instead, he or she will accept their excuses and adopt a problem-solving approach. The therapist will suggest that maybe they could try a different time, a different day, a different activity, or a different baby-sitter and then suggest that they try again.

When the therapist continues to focus on the assignment, the couple will begin to take it more seriously and will begin to take more active steps to do it. Sometimes they do so in order to avoid the embarrassment of telling the therapist that they did not do their homework. When the assignment yields positive results, they begin to find their own reasons to spend time together.

Going Out to Dinner: Joan and Steve

Joan and Steve have few common interests. Steve goes to sporting events with his friends and Joan goes to the theater with her friends.

The therapist and couple begin to focus on companionship activities. The therapist wonders what they might want to do together. After much discussion, they decide on going out to dinner. Follow up at the next session reveals they have not done it. Therapist probing elicits excuses. They could not find a baby-sitter and were tired. The therapist continues to suggest that they go out to dinner and repeats the rationale: It will allow them to enjoy each other's company.

Follow up at the next session reveals that a crisis with the kids prevented them from doing it. However, they indicated that they did go for a walk together. "How was that?" the therapist inquires. It had its good and bad moments. During the walk, Joan shared the events of her day and Steve appeared interested. Steve was less vocal about his day, but said he enjoyed hearing his wife discuss her day. The down side of the experience was that Steve likes to walk faster than Joan and they argued about it. The therapist wondered aloud, "What was the goal of the walk, exercise or togetherness?" They agreed it was togetherness and that Steve would slow down. The therapist wondered whether walking together was a better companionship activity than going out to dinner. They agreed it probably was.

During the next session the therapist inquired about their walks. They said that they did continue them and had enjoyed each other's company. "How so?" the therapist asked. Joan said that she appreciated having Steve's undivided attention. The therapist probed Steve's experience and asked if this felt burdensome. He said it did not. They reported another companionship activity. Steve needed a suit for work and they went shopping together. Steve appreciated Joan's help picking out the suit. They also had lunch together afterward.

Their interaction during the session appeared more relaxed. There was more smiling and laughter. As the sessions continued, the therapist kept the companionship issue on the table and inquired about planned and spontaneous companionship activities. Questions about those activities continued to be, "What was it like?" and "Did it allow you to feel closer?"

ENCOURAGING NONSEXUAL TOUCHING AND SEXUAL INTIMACY

Nonsexual Touching

Nonsexual physical touch is a powerful means for spouses to feel closer to each other. For many couples there has been little touching, stroking, hugging, or kissing. They do not rub each other's back, feet, or shoulders in nonsexual ways to relieve tension.

The therapist will suggest that in order to begin feeling closer to each other, they resume these activities. For example, they can hold hands or snuggle when they are watching TV together. If they used to give one another back rubs, they could begin to do so again.

As with other assignments, the therapist will follow up. Did they do the touching assignment? Did it allow them to feel closer to each other? If they did not follow through with the assignment, the therapist will probe for obstacles and look for ways to help them overcome them.

Sexual Intimacy

When they come in for therapy, many spouses have ceased to have a sexual relationship. They often do not sleep in the same bed, or in the same room, thus the intimacy of seeing each other undressing or naked is absent. The pleasure of a sexual relationship is also absent.

Wanting more affection and a more active sex life is often explicitly stated by spouses as a goal for therapy. Even when it is not stated directly, most spouses desire this. When it is absent, the relationship feels incomplete. They feel more like roommates than lovers.

Self-esteem issues are activated when there is no affection, touching, or sex. Spouses want to feel desired by their partners. They feel undesirable and unlovable when their partners show no interest in them.

Probing to Understand Their Prior Sexual Experiences

The therapist will want to understand their prior sexual history. What have they experienced with each other in the past? Was their sexual relationship satisfying or were there problems from the beginning? Probing will elicit the spouses' feelings of satisfaction with their earlier sexual relationship or the ways in which they have been disappointed or felt exploited.

One frequent pattern is for one spouse to be disappointed in their sex life and to have lost interest in sex. The partner is likely to have repeatedly initiated sex and been rejected by the disinterested partner. The initiator is now unwilling to become vulnerable and be rejected again.

What do they want now? The therapist will inquire about what happens physically and sexually now. What are the sleeping arrangements? Do they sleep in the same bed or in the same bedroom? Is one or the other a light sleeper? Are there snoring problems? When did they last have sex? Was it enjoyable? Was it difficult?

Encouraging Sex: Setting the Stage and Discussing Obstacles

Consider the following example. Steve and Joan have rarely had sex in the past few years. Joan felt that Steve had been sexually selfish earlier in their marriage. Eventually she lost interest and began to reject Steve's sexual advances. Steve acknowledged that early in their relationship he had not paid enough attention to Joan's sexual needs. However, he believes he has changed and this is no longer true.

Steve has his own issues with Joan. He believes that Joan withheld sex as means of controlling him, and he harbors resentment about this. Now he is wary about again putting himself in a position where he will feel rejected and controlled.

Despite their misgivings, Steve and Joan both want to resume a more active sex life. Joan misses the closeness and the sexual pleasure she did at times experience with Steve. She also wants to feel desired again. Steve too misses their sex life and wants an interested sexual partner.

Protecting the Initiating Partner from Rejection

In order to break their impasse, the therapist emphasizes the importance of risk taking and creates a coordinated assignment. Despite the fear, someone needs to take the risk and initiate sex. A scenario is created where the initiator, in this case Steve, will be protected from rejection. To accomplish this the therapist needs to probe for obstacles that would lead Joan to reject him.

THERAPIST: [To Joan] If he suggests having sex, it is important that you are receptive. What might get in the way of your being receptive?

JOAN: If I haven't felt close to him or am mad at him, then I am not interested.

THERAPIST: [To Steve] Can you tell when she is mad about something?

STEVE: She usually is mad about something.

THERAPIST: Maybe at one time that was true, but not now. Can you tell when she is mad?

STEVE: I usually can tell.

THERAPIST: Can you tell when she is in a good mood?

STEVE: Yeah.

THERAPIST: What about the feeling close part? She needs to feel a connection with you in order to be interested in sex.

STEVE: Lately there have been times when I have felt close to her. I don't know what she is feeling.

THERAPIST: [To Joan] Are there times when you are feeling close to Steve?

JOAN: Yeah.

THERAPIST: How would he know when they are?

JOAN: He could ask me.

THERAPIST: Could you see yourself asking her?

STEVE: I have never done that, but I suppose I could.

THERAPIST: So what would you say to her?

STEVE: I don't know.

THERAPIST: [To Joan] Do you have any ideas?

JOAN: He could say, "Are you feeling okay about us?"

The therapist continues to discuss what needs to happen to ensure that the initiating partner will not experience rejection. Later in the session the therapist probes to find out what Steve says to initiate sex. How difficult is it for Steve to do this? Are his choice of words off-putting to Joan?

THERAPIST: What do you say to initiate sex?

STEVE: I don't know. Do you want to go upstairs? Something like that.

THERAPIST: What is it like for you to say that?

STEVE: It is hard.

THERAPIST: How so?

STEVE: I just don't like to be that direct.

The therapist and Steve discuss his discomfort with directness. Joan is listening. Hopefully she is learning something about what goes on within him. She needs to understand how the past pattern of rejection has contributed to their current sexual impasse.

The therapist then asks more about when they have sex. When is it most likely to occur? During the week? In the morning? On the weekend? What might enhance the mood? Do they light candles, play music, use lotions? Then the therapist turns to Joan's part in the coordinated assignment. She must be prepared not to rebuff Steve's sexual overtures.

THERAPIST: [To Joan] I hear you saying you want him to initiate sex.
JOAN: I am not going to beg him. He needs to show he is interested.
THERAPIST: [To Joan] Are you ready to be responsive when he does?

The therapist and couple continue to discuss potential obstacles and ways to overcome them.

Following Up

Dealing with Obstacles If the Assignment Is Avoided

When following up, the therapist will ask, "How did it go as far as sex is concerned?" Quite likely, sex will not have occurred. Perhaps they had an argument, or had a hectic week, or were busy with the kids, or were too tired. The therapist will accept their excuses and persevere.

If they have had an argument, the therapist will process it. If other issues emerged, they will discuss them. The therapist will then return to the sexual assignment. Had Steve been thinking about having sex? Had Joan? It will often emerge that both had been thinking about it.

The therapist will probe and elicit more about what went on internally within each. It may turn out there had been an opportunity for them to be together sexually. Steve may have been interested but thought Joan was not. The therapist will probe. Did Joan remember that night? Was she interested that night? It may turn out that she had been; however, since Steve said nothing, she assumed he was not.

The therapist asks Joan if she would have been receptive had he asked. She says she would have been. Additional probing reveals that Joan had been feeling good about Steve that night. Earlier, he had been helpful with something important to her and she was appreciative. Steve is surprised to learn of this. He thought she seemed irritable that night. She is surprised to hear that. "It sounds like you don't read each other well, and that each is more interested in sex than the other thinks," the therapist observes.

At some point during the next session the therapist asks, "What is going on sexually?" Perhaps they will have had sex, perhaps not. The therapist will process whatever emerges.

Probing for Positive Consequences When Sex Happens

Eventually the couple will have a sexual encounter. The therapist will inquire about the experience. How did it come about? Who initiated it? Was it enjoyable? Did they feel closer to each other? If it was enjoyable and they do feel closer, it is often obvious in their nonverbal behavior. They are softer with each other, they may smile or laugh more, make more eye contact, touch each other more, or use endearing phrases.

Although the barriers are temporarily down, they may not stay down. The therapist must keep the sexual issue on the table.

Processing Negative Sexual Experiences

If sex did happen and the experience was negative, the therapist will want to process what happened. Was one or the other uptight, distracted, and unable to focus on his or her own enjoyment? Was the spouse frustrated with a partner who seemed unaware of his or her needs? Did they argue over who should be doing what?

The therapist will probe for the experience of each and deal with their sexual frustrations. Serving in the gatekeeper role, the therapist will probe, convey the perspectives of one to the other, and engage in problem solving.

As the sessions progress the therapist will keep the sexual issue on the table and ask, "How are things going sexually?"

Chapter 10

Accepting Partner Differences and Limitations

Relationships derive energy from differences. Spouses typically do not choose to live with clones of themselves. Although doing so might cut down on conflict, stagnation would also result. Individuals choose to marry others who will fill in their gaps or who will be receptacles for disowned parts of themselves. Introverts are attracted to extroverts; cautious types to more spontaneous partners; emotionally restricted spouses to more openly affectionate partners; thinking types to feeling types; undisciplined individuals to those with self-control; conventional types to rebels; protectors to those needing protection. These differences serve to counterbalance excesses and bring completeness to the relationship.

DIFFERENCES AS AN IRRITANT

Unfortunately, for spouses in distressed marriages, the differences that were once an attraction are now a constant irritant. Knowing that one's spouse is different in fundamental ways can mean giving up cherished hopes about the marriage. Awareness that the partner does not share the spouse's values, view of the world, or coping style sometimes increases the experience of loneliness.

Spouses will resist knowing the inner experience of their partners if they dislike what they come to understand. Wives who have been raised to value caring for the feelings of others are often appalled by their husbands' insensitivity to others. Husbands who have been raised to value independence are often appalled by their wives willingness to be influenced by others. If a wife accepts her husband's sensitivity to criticism, she may have to give up not only her freedom to criticize him, but also her unrealistic view of him as the strong, invulnerable protector. Trying to force the partner to change becomes a repetitive theme and a source of power struggles.

LEARNING TO ACCEPT DIFFERENCES AND LIMITATIONS

The therapist interventions described in the earlier chapters are intended to effect change. Spouses are encouraged to engage in prosocial behavior to improve the relationship. After attempts at change are made, and hopefully some improvement has occurred, the therapist may shift the focus to helping spouses accept things that will not change.

Often the changes a spouse wants the partner to make are unrealistic. Accepting what "is" can reduce power struggles and unhappiness over partner characteristics that are unlikely to change. The therapist may suggest that some of the partner's characteristics are based on fundamental gender or temperament characteristics that are unlikely to change. A more pragmatic approach is to accept the partner's limitations and decide how to cope with them.

Consider the following therapist interventions.

Introversion

A husband has made efforts to be become more helpful and involved with his wife and family. However, his wife still complains about his tendency to withdraw. The therapist believes that the degree of change that has occurred is the full extent of change of which the husband is capable. Rather than continue to be disappointed, the therapist thinks it would help the wife to accept her husband as he is.

WIFE: He spends so much time working in the basement.
THERAPIST: I think he is trying to be more involved with you, but by temperament he is introverted. His capacity to interact with others is limited. It is a core part of who he is. I don't think we can change that.

Rigidity

A wife complains about her husband's rigid expectations and demands. He has made successful efforts to become more flexible; however, he remains a fairly rigid individual.

WIFE: [Angrily] He gets upset about the smallest thing. The toys must be lined up in the cabinet. The dishes have special places to go in the dishwasher. The newspaper must be folded neatly and put on the coffee table.

THERAPIST: I know it is frustrating. I think it is sad that he is this way. I don't think he likes it any more than you do. I think you need to see his rigidity as his problem and figure out how you are going to cope with it without getting upset.

Fears

A wife's fears restrict the couple's activities. When the husband attempts to force her to overcome her fears, power struggles result. The therapist wants the husband to accept that her fears will not be overcome by coercion.

HUSBAND: We don't garden because she is afraid of Lyme disease. We don't run together because she is afraid of dogs.

THERAPIST: You try to pressure her into these things as though she really isn't afraid. It won't work. If you accept her the way she is and stop pressuring her, perhaps she will want to work on these things on her own.

Somatization

A wife is overly preoccupied with her bodily ailments. The husband complains about her constant visits to doctors. When he criticizes her, she defends herself and they engage in power struggles.

HUSBAND: She runs off to a doctor whenever something hurts. It gets ridiculous.

THERAPIST: She is highly sensitive to pain. She gets preoccupied with her pain and can't shake it off. You can. She can't. How long has she been this way?

HUSBAND: Ever since I have known her.

THERAPIST: So you have been trying to get her to change for twenty years. Has she changed?

HUSBAND: No.

THERAPIST: Maybe you would be better off accepting her the way she is. Arguing about this is like banging your head against the wall until it bleeds. The wall is still there.

Bragging

A wife is infuriated that her husband is always calling attention to himself and showing off.

WIFE: He has to show off constantly. He has to show everybody the new riding mower he just bought. He has to brag about how much our pool cost. I am not like that.

THERAPIST: I know you are not like that, but he is different from you. He is a more materially oriented person than you are. Talking about these things gives him pleasure. Whatever the reason, I think you are better off accepting that part of him. It is part of who he is.

ACCEPTING GENDER DIFFERENCES

Power struggles over gender differences are pervasive in distressed marriages. Although the spouses may not identify their struggle as related to gender, they will argue constantly about who should be more or less caring, self-reliant, emotional, or involved. Consider the following discussion of a husband's behavior.

Accepting the Husband's Achievement Orientation

Wives who place primacy on the marital relationship will interpret their husband's solitary behavior as rejection. The therapist's role is often to help the wife accept her husband's autonomy and achievement orientation. The therapist may suggest that the wife is pursuing her needs through affiliation while her husband is pursuing his needs through achievement. This may be presented as an unintentional clash of spousal needs. The husband's need to pursue work objectives often is *not avoidance or rejection,* but instead reflects his orientation toward the world.

WIFE: All he thinks or cares about is his work. He doesn't care about me.
THERAPIST: I think he cares about you. However, he needs to work hard and succeed in order to feel good about himself.
WIFE: But it shouldn't mean everything.
THERAPIST: Think of it this way: How would you feel if your mother or your children became ill and you were not there for them?
WIFE: Awful, guilty.
THERAPIST: That is how he feels if his work is not going well. It is frightening to him. He is afraid he might fail.
WIFE: That is ridiculous. Work is just a way to support your family.
THERAPIST: Many men do define themselves by their success at work. Maybe someday that will change, but for now, I think it would help you if you understood and accepted that part of him.

As the sessions proceed, the therapist will reiterate the basic message: You will be less frustrated with your partner if you accept the things you cannot change.

A CASE HISTORY

Chapter 11

The Marriage of Sam and Diane

INTRODUCTION

Sam and Diane met at a business conference. Both had been married previously and Diane had a son, Jimmy. They began to see each other often and soon married. After marrying, their relationship became traditional in that Sam became the breadwinner while Diane stayed home and took care of the house and her child.

When presenting for therapy, Sam was angry. He felt Diane ignored what was important to him. Order and cleanliness were important to Sam and often Diane did not do laundry, left dishes in the sink, and left food on the kitchen table. When things were not orderly, Sam would get agitated and become critical of Diane.

Several triangular issues were present. Sam believed that Diane indulged Jimmy and blocked him from being an active parent. Sam was suspicious when Diane saw her ex-husband and excluded him. He was also angry that Diane talked to her sister about their marital problems.

Sam had other concerns as well. He felt burdened by the amount of attention that Diane seemed to require. Her demands for his attention seemed endless. He was angry that Diane kept pressuring him to get a dog when he was opposed it. He was also angry that Diane frequently rejected him when he initiated sex.

Diane's affect when presenting for therapy was a mixture of anger, depression, and anxiety. Diane felt besieged by Sam's anger. It scared her and caused her to be uptight around him. Diane also had her own resentments. She resented Sam's criticism of her spending habits. Having no income of her own, she felt controlled by him and expressed her resentment in passive-aggressive ways. She was also angry that she could not depend on Sam to take care of Jimmy. The last time she left them alone, Sam forgot to help Jimmy with his homework. Diane also had security and rejection concerns. She thought that Sam could find time to be with his friends but could not find time to be with her.

Both seemed disillusioned with their marriage and doubted that they could ever get along. Sam and Diane's pattern of marital distress followed the less common pattern of the husband feeling disregarded, angry, and critical. In the early sessions Diane was encouraged to be more responsive to her husband, whereas Sam was encouraged to monitor and control his anger. Although this pattern is seen less frequently, it demonstrates the typical support-focused marital therapy interventions.

SESSIONS ONE THROUGH EIGHTEEN

Session One

The therapist engaged in empathic probing to elicit their concerns about the relationship. The couple described their arguments over the condition of the house. Sam was visibly angry at Diane during the session and Diane appeared intimidated and defensive. She said Sam was too uptight, and she wished he could be more laid back.

Before the session ended, the therapist asked each what they wanted to achieve in therapy. Sam expressed his desire that Diane do a better job with the housework. Diane wanted Sam to be less angry. She also wanted him spend more time with her.

The therapist understood one of their destructive patterns and presented it to them. The therapist suggested to Diane that when she let the housework slide, Sam became angry. The therapist suggested to Sam that when he became angry and accusatory, Diane became defensive rather than improving her housekeeping. The therapist suggested that their goals were connected. Diane could achieve her own goal (less anger from Sam) by addressing his goal (a more organized and orderly house). Sam could achieve his goal (a more orderly house) by trying to monitor and control his anger, thereby protecting Diane from defensiveness. The therapist gave them an assignment, suggesting that in the intervening week Sam could work on controlling his anger and Diane could work on her housework.

The therapist ended the session by describing the couple's tasks and the therapist's tasks. On the way out, Sam was still angry. He was not hopeful about marital therapy.

Session Two

Much of the session was devoted to discussing Diane's unhappiness about the amount of time Sam spent at work and with his friends. Sam would go to happy hour after work and would not return home until late. The therapist conveyed Diane's perspective to Sam and tried to help Sam understand how she felt rejected when he came home late. The therapist began problem solving by probing for what each felt was an appropriate time for Sam to be home after work. They agreed that being home by 7 p.m. was acceptable. The therapist probed for obstacles and wondered if Sam would feel controlled by this. Sam said he did not think so.

Diane raised the spending issue. When they were shopping together, Diane bought a blouse. Sam complained that she was wasting money. Diane thought that was ridiculous. She said she resented his constant monitoring of her spending. The therapist presented the destructive pattern and suggested to Sam that Diane's resentment over this issue made it more difficult for her to want to please him, for example, by doing the housework. Probing elicited that Sam was afraid that Diane's spending would put them in debt. As they discussed the issue, it emerged that Diane was actually frugal in her spending. The therapist suggested that Sam try to refrain from commenting on her spending. Buying a new blouse was unlikely to put them in debt and buying it would allow Diane to feel less controlled.

The therapist again focused on what they wanted to achieve in therapy. Diane reiterated that Sam's anger was a problem for her. Sam reiterated that he thought that Diane ignored what was important to him.

The therapist inquired about the assignments from Session one and asked Diane how she was doing with housekeeping and repeated the rationale: It would reduce Sam's anger. The therapist asked Sam if he was working on controlling his anger and repeated the rationale: It would make Diane less fearful and defensive. Both indicated that they had taken his suggestions seriously and were working at them. The therapist's impression was that they were committed to therapy and were working at it.

The therapist suggested a companionship activity. He suggested that they find a baby-sitter and go out together. This was met with a strained silence. Probing elicited that Diane was afraid that if they went out together they would fight. Sam said he did not want to be the one to take the initiative and plan it. The therapist decided it was too soon for companionship assignments. The therapist ended the session by indicating that the following two sessions would be devoted to obtaining their individual histories.

Session Three

This was an individual session with Sam. In addition to obtaining his personal history and view of the marriage, the therapist used the session to follow up on previous assignments. Sam indicated that he was trying to be less critical and angry. He indicated that he was coming home before 7 p.m. and noticed that it helped reduce the tension.

The therapist also used the opportunity to discuss the spending issue by reiterating that Diane felt resentful of his constant monitoring of her spending. It caused her to feel controlled and made her less eager to be responsive to him.

Session Four

This was an individual session with Diane. In addition to obtaining her personal history and view of the marriage, the therapist followed up on previous assignments. Diane indicated that she was trying harder with the housework and thought that it was helping. The therapist used the opportunity to convey to Diane the importance of this issue to Sam and his sense of agitation when the house was disorderly.

Session Five

The couple and therapist were reunited after the individual sessions. The therapist chose not to make a formal presentation of their marital problems, and instead to pick up where they had left off.

The couple reported that the relationship was better. Diane was trying to improve her housework and Sam was openly appreciative. The therapist used the opportunity to reiterate the pattern and suggested that she could control his anger by doing what was important to him, i.e., the housework.

Diane raised the issue of getting a dog. Sam expressed anger that she keeps bringing this issue up since he has told her repeatedly that he hates dogs. To him, this is an example of how she disregards him.

The therapist commented to Diane that she appears to plow ahead without any concern for Sam's feelings and suggested that this is how she creates the anger that she so dislikes. The therapist suggested that when making this decision the feelings of both spouses need to be considered.

Session Six

Diane expressed her unhappiness that Sam had isolated himself in front of the computer and did not talk to her. Therapist probing led to an emotional self-disclosure from Sam. Sam said he feels overwhelmed by the amount of attention Diane craves and doubts he can ever meet her need for attention. He said this keeps him from getting closer to Diane. Hearing this, Diane became upset and tearful, as did Sam.

The focus switched to companionship activities. Both appeared to miss doing fun activities together. Sam wanted them to go to the movies. Diane wanted them to go to museums and for walks in the park. When they discussed this, obstacles emerged. Diane said going to the movies bothered her. She felt claustrophobic in theaters and listening to the people around her crunching on popcorn bothered her. Sam said that museums bored him and that he preferred staying home.

The therapist used the opportunity to present the support model. Speaking to Diane, the therapist said, "If going to the movies means a lot to Sam, you should find a way to overcome your discomfort and do it. That way he feels you care about what is important to him." The therapist probed to determine how she might feel more comfortable in theaters. They decided they would try to find seats away from others.

The therapist probed Sam's boredom in museums. It emerged that he was only mildly bored with museums and indicated that he was willing to go if it was important to Diane. The therapist reiterated that doing so would allow her to feel that he cared about what is important to her. The therapist reiterated the basic message: When you take your partner seriously, and respond to what is important to your partner, then the relationship will be better between you.

Session Seven

The early interventions appeared to have had an effect. They reported that the relationship was much better. From Diane's perspective it was 60 to 70 percent better. From Sam's perspective it was 50 percent better.

Therapist inquiry elicited that they did go to a movie together; however, it had not gone well. Diane was restless and did not enjoy it. They had not gone to a museum or for a walk in the park. The therapist inquired about the housework and anger assignments. Both reported they had been trying and each was aware of the other's efforts. Diane appeared less depressed. She said that they were now able to discuss issues without arguing. Sam's attempts to control his anger appeared to be paying off.

Much of the session was devoted to discussing a parenting issue. Sam felt Diane indulged Jimmy and would give in when he became demanding. Diane became defensive and counterattacked. She criticized Sam's negligence with Jimmy. She complained that he wanted to be a more involved parent but that she could not trust him with basic things, such as helping Jimmy with homework. The therapist intervened to prevent escalation. He initiated a discussion with Diane about discipline and limits. Probing elicited that Diane knew she should be firmer with Jimmy; however, she finds it difficult to say "no." The therapist empathized with her dilemma and then reframed the situation by suggesting that a good mother sometimes must take painful steps such as saying "no" and adhering to limits. This was in the best interest of the child. Diane was upset but appeared to be listening.

The therapist then initiated a conversation with Sam. Probing elicited that he felt remorse for having forgotten to help Jimmy with his homework. He said he would not allow such a thing to happen again. Both seemed distressed when the session ended.

Session Eight

This was another difficult session. There had been backsliding regarding Diane's housekeeping and Sam was angry. After processing the material, the therapist again presented the pattern: When she was good about her housekeeping, the relationship went well; when she was not, there were arguments.

The therapist inquired about how she was doing with saying "no" to Jimmy. She said she was trying but that it was difficult.

Sam raised the issue of Diane's seeing her ex-husband for lunch. Diane was defensive. The therapist suggested that seeing her ex-husband made Sam suspicious and this was not good for their marriage. The therapist then suggested to Sam that if Diane did not get the attention she craved from Sam, she would look for it elsewhere. This led to a discussion of why they are unable to engage in more companionship activities. They had gone to the movies once and had gone to a museum once, but nothing more came of it. In probing for obstacles, it appeared that each rejects the other's companionship ideas and they remain stuck. Both left the session upset.

Session Nine

The therapist reviewed the couple's progress in therapy. Despite the emotionally upsetting nature of the last several sessions, they appear to have made progress. Diane is keeping the house organized and Sam is trying to handle his anger more constructively. Rather than get angry, when he sees a mess in the house he now tries to be lighthearted and make a joke about it. He has also backed off about monitoring Diane's spending.

The therapist raised the issue of Diane seeing her ex-husband. Diane acknowledged that this was creating a marital problem. She reluctantly agreed that she would resist such meetings in the future.

Session Ten

A triangular issue emerged. Diane often calls her sister and tells her about their marital problems. This angers Sam, who feels "tattled on." The therapist attempted to convey Sam's perspective to Diane by describing the sense of shame Sam felt knowing her sister was aware of their marital problems. Diane could see Sam's distress and began to grasp his perspective. She agreed that when she talked to her sister, she would not share the details of their marital problems. Sam appeared relieved.

Sessions Eleven Through Fifteen

Sessions eleven through fifteen dealt with the problems described previously. There was progress and backsliding with regard to Diane's housework and Sam controlling his anger. The therapist continued to take the perspective of each, present patterns, problem solve, assign homework, and follow through.

Session Sixteen

The relationship appeared to be going well. During the session Sam played with Diane's hair. They touched, kissed each other's hands, and sat closer together.

Session Seventeen

The session dealt with their sexual pattern. Diane's sex drive is lower than Sam's. When Sam suggests sex Diane often says, "I am not in the mood," and he feels rejected. This concerns Diane, who understands how important sex is to Sam. She does not like rejecting him; however, she finds it difficult to get in the mood, particularly when Sam has ignored her all night.

Therapist probing elicited that Diane has trouble relaxing. When she asks Sam to help her get in the mood by sitting together on the sofa and rubbing her back he resents it.

Problem solving led to the following approach. In order to prevent rejection, instead of saying "I am not in the mood," Diane will say, "Help me get in the mood." In order to deal with Sam's resentment the therapist reframed the issue by suggesting that women need more time to become relaxed and sexually aroused. The therapist also said that many spouses are easily distracted by intrusive thoughts and need more time to rid themselves of the distractions. Sam agreed that he will try to overcome his resentment and will sit with her and help her relax by rubbing her back.

Session Eighteen

The therapist followed up on the sexual assignment. Diane reported that she was able to say "Help me get in the mood" and Sam did sit with her and rub her back. However, the assignment had been only partly successful. She still had trouble relaxing. This led to a discussion of how difficult it was for Diane to communicate about what she wants sexually. After much reluctance she revealed that she disliked the way Sam kisses. Sam was upset to hear this; however, he was willing to listen. They agreed they would experiment with different ways of kissing.

SUBSEQUENT SESSIONS

In subsequent sessions Sam and Diane continued to deal with the problems discussed previously. Housework, Diane's spending, triangular issues, and Sam's anger all began to lose their power to upset them. They began to spontaneously engage in more companionship activities and their sexual relationship improved. They also began to accept each other's differences. Diane became reconciled to the idea that Sam did not like dogs. Sam became reconciled to the idea that, although Diane was trying, she would never be an enthusiastic housekeeper. After twenty-five sessions, both felt better about their relationship than they ever had.

THE OUTCOME STUDY

Chapter 12
Assessing the Effectiveness of Support-Focused Marital Therapy

Robert P. Rugel
Jacqueline R. Shapo

STUDY ONE:
THE SUPPORT-FOCUSED MARITAL THERAPY WAITLIST-CONTROL COMPARISON

In the present study the effectiveness of support-focused marital therapy (SFMT) was determined by comparing couples treated with support-focused marital therapy with couples who were assigned to a waitlist-control group.

Jacqueline Raznik Shapo was born in Detroit, Michigan. She holds a BA in psychology from the University of Michigan (1988), a JD from the University of Michigan Law School (1990), and an MA in psychology from George Mason University (2000). She expects to receive her PhD from George Mason University's Clinical Psychology program in 2004. During her years of legal practice in Illinois, Michigan, and Virginia, Ms. Shapo was particularly interested in theory and practice of negotiation and finds many related skills helpful in her clinical work with couples. She looks forward to continuing her research and clinical work with couples and families.

Method

Participants

Participants responded to a newspaper advertisement seeking couples interested in marital therapy. To be included in the study, the Spanier Dyadic Adjustment Scale score of one spouse had to be below 100. Couples were excluded if their primary problem was substance addiction, physical abuse, or an ongoing extramarital affair. Four couples were excluded on this basis. Couples who met the criteria were informed of the research nature of the study, signed a standard consent form, and were randomly assigned to the treatment or waitlist-control groups. Fourteen couples dropped out of the study prior to the completion of the treatment or the waitlist period. Of these, seven were in the treatment group, six were in the control group and one couple was not classified. A chi-square test indicated that the difference in dropouts between the two groups was not significant ($X^2 = .077, p = .782$).

After accounting for dropouts, 22 couples remained in the treatment group and 21 couples remained in the control group. The demographic information on the spouses in the treatment and waitlist-control conditions can be seen in Table 12.1.

Measures

Dyadic Adjustment Scale (DAS) (Spanier, 1976). The DAS is widely used as a measure of marital satisfaction and change in satisfaction following marital therapy. It is a Likert-type self-report questionnaire that provides an overall assessment of marital satisfaction. An internal consistency of .96 has been reported (Spanier, 1976). Validity evidence is reported in Corcoran and Fischer (1987).

Areas of Change Questionnaire (ACQ) (Weiss, Hops, and Patterson, 1973). This is a self-report measure that asks how much change the respondent would like from the partner in 34 specific areas of marital behavior. It successfully discriminates between distressed and nondistressed couples and scores have shown expected changes as a function of therapy (Margolin and Fernandez, 1983). A single

TABLE 12.1. Demographic Variables

Variable	SFMT Husbands M	(SD)	SFMT Wives M	(SD)	Waitlist-Control Husbands M	(SD)	Waitlist-Control Wives M	(SD)
Age	45.6	(9.7)	42.7	(9.3)	45.4	(11.2)	43.8	(11.7)
Years dated	2.2	(2.3)	2.3	(2.3)	2.7	(2.2)	2.9	(2.3)
Years married	13.8	(10.4)	13.8	(10.4)	13.9	(12.3)	13.9	(12.3)
Previous marriages	.18	(.39)	.18	(.39)	.29	(.64)	.24	(.44)
Level of education*	3.2	(1.2)	3.0	(1.4)	3.3	(1.2)	3.0	(1.5)
Individual income**	69.5	(28.7)	37.7	(30.2)	74.5	(45.3)	32.6	(29.3)
Children in household	1.5	(1.3)	1.5	(1.3)	1.8	(1.2)	1.8	(1.2)
Children not in household	.55	(1.0)	.36	(.85)	.86	(1.4)	.85	(1.4)

* 1 = high school degree; 2 = two-year degree; 3 = college degree; 4 = master's degree; 5 = PhD or JD

** In thousands of dollars

M = Mean
SD = Standard deviation

score is derived for each participant across the content areas, with high scores indicating greater desire for partner change.

SCL-90-R (Derogatis, 1989). This is a measure of psychopathology. It consists of a 90-item Likert-type self-report symptom inventory. Adequate reliability and validity evidence is reported in Derogatis (1989). Total SCL-90-R raw scores were used in the present analyses with larger numbers indicating greater overall psychopathology.

Spielberger Trait Anger Inventory (STAI) (Spielberger et al., 1983). This measure consists of a ten-item Likert-type self-report scale that assesses how frequently a person feels anger over time and how many situations are perceived as anger provoking. Adequate reliability and validity information is provided in Spielberger et al. (1983).

Rosenberg Self-Esteem Inventory (RSE) (Rosenberg, 1965). This is a widely used measure of global self-esteem that consists of ten Likert-type self-report items. Adequate reliability and validity evidence is reported in Rosenberg (1989).

Therapists

Six therapists participated in the study. Four of the therapists were enrolled in the doctoral clinical psychology training program at George Mason University. Most had more than two years of clinical training and most had more than six months of supervised psychotherapy training. Two of the therapists had recently graduated from the program and had doctoral degrees in clinical psychology. The therapists were all considered novices at marital therapy as most had little or no prior experience in dealing with couples prior to the study.

Therapist training included didactic instruction in use of the treatment manual, observation of training tapes, and weekly group supervision. Individual supervision was also conducted as needed. All therapists received roughly the same amount of training. All supervision was provided by the first author, who also reviewed audiotapes of all sessions to assess adherence to the manual. Each therapist was also required to fill out a seven-item "adherence to the manual" form after each session.

Procedure

All couples were administered the outcome measures at a qualifying interview prior to the beginning of treatment or the waitlist period. For the treatment group, prior to the beginning of session 12, the outcome measures were readministered and were followed by the last treatment session. For the waitlist-control group, the outcome measures were readministered after 12 weeks in the waitlist condition.

Results

Randomization

A nonparametric Runs test confirmed that the order of group assignment to the treatment and waitlist-control groups did not differ significantly from chance ($Z = .31$, $p > .75$).

Demographic Variables

Two separate MANOVAs, for husbands and wives respectively, revealed no significant treatment versus waitlist-control differences on the nine demographic variables ($F_{9,33} = .84$, $p > .58$, $F_{9,33} = .48$, $p > .88$).

Chi-square tests revealed no group differences based on race. Comparisons revealed three husbands in the SFMT group were nonwhite and two husbands in the control group were nonwhite ($X^2 = .18, p > .67$). Similar analysis revealed four wives in the SFMT group were nonwhite and two wives in the control group were nonwhite ($X^2 = .67, p > .41$) Groups also did not differ significantly in the number of interracial couples. In the SFMT group, five couples were interracial as compared to two couples in the waitlist-control group ($X^2 = 1.37, p > .24$).

Pretreatment Measures

Two separate MANOVAs, for husbands and wives respectively, revealed no significant differences in initial scores between the SFMT and the waitlist-control groups on the DAS, ACQ, STAI, SCL-90-R, or the RSE ($F_{5,37} = 1.40, p > .24; F_{5,37} = .89, p > .49$).

T-tests were conducted using the combined treatment and waitlist-control samples to determine whether husbands and wives differed on the five measures prior to the intervention. The results indicated that, prior to treatment, wives had higher scores on the ACQ, indicating more desired partner change, than husbands ($t(42) = 3.41, p < .001$); wives also exhibited more pretherapy anger than their husbands on the STAI ($t(42) = -2.25, p < .03$).

Change As a Function of Treatment: The Support-Focused Marital Therapy Group versus the Waitlist-Control Group

Because the DAS and ACQ were targeted to measure the spouses' experience of the marital satisfaction, whereas the SCL-90-R, the STAI, and the RSE were targeted to measure individual distress, two separate, doubly repeated MANOVA analyses were run: one for the marital satisfaction measures and one for the individual distress measures.

Measures of Marital Satisfaction. Use of a doubly repeated measures MANOVA enabled examination of group, time, gender, and interaction effects, while having the advantage of keeping the partners paired with each other.

The key effect tested in the analysis was the time-by-group interaction, which indicated whether the SFMT and waitlist-control groups changed in different ways in their mean level of marital satisfaction from pretest to posttest. A significant time × group interaction was found, indicating that the SFMT was superior to the waitlist-control group at posttreatment although there were no differences at pretreatment ($F_{2,40} = 3.48, p < .04$). A significant overall effect for time was also found ($F_{2,40} = 4.75, p < .01$); however, time effects are typically not interpretable where a significant time-by-group interaction occurs.

The analysis also revealed a significant overall effect for gender ($F_{2,40} = 8.55, p < .01$), consistent with the pretreatment analysis indicating that wives were less satisfied with their marriages at pretest and posttest. The group did not interact with gender ($F_{2,40} = 2.36, p > .11$), and gender did not interact with time ($F_{2,40} = .21, p > .81$). There was no time × gender × group interaction, indicating that the interventions affected both husbands and wives similarly ($F = .18, p > .84$).

Follow-up univariate analyses for the time × group interaction showed significant effects on both the DAS ($F_{1,41} = 4.70, p < .04$) and the ACQ ($F_{1,41} = 5.99, p < .02$). An examination of the means in Table 12.2 reveals that the SFMT group experienced a significantly greater increase in marital satisfaction (as measured by the DAS) and significantly decreased number of desired changes in the relationship (as measured by the ACQ) following treatment, as compared with the control group.

Measures of Individual Distress. The doubly repeated measures MANOVA on the measures SCL-90-R, STAI, and RSE revealed no significant time × group interaction ($F_{3,39} = .37, p > .78$); there was a significant overall effect for time ($F_{3,39} = 7.69, p < .01$), indicating that both groups improved with the passage of time and that SFMT yielded no additional effect. Further, no overall group differences across assessment times were observed ($F_{3,39} = .84, p > .48$), and the analysis revealed no overall effects for gender ($F_{3,39} = 2.06, p > .12$), group × gender ($F_{3,39} = 1.44, p > .25$), gender × time ($F_{3,39} = 1.01, p > .40$) or time × gender × group ($F_{3,39} = .70, p > .56$).

Separate Analysis for Husbands and Wives

Group effects were also analyzed separately for husbands and wives using two repeated measures MANOVAs. Means are shown in Table 12.2. When examined alone, husbands demonstrated a significant multivariate time × group interaction ($F_{2,40} = 3.62, p < .04$) on the

TABLE 12.2. Pretreatment and Posttreatment Scores

	SFMT				Waitlist-Control			
	Pretreatment		Posttreatment		Pretreatment		Posttreatment	
	M	(SD)	M	(SD)	M	(SD)	M	(SD)
Husbands								
DAS	83.77	(14.61)	90.41	(13.90)	91.00	(13.77)	90.76	(15.97)
ACQ	13.05	(6.08)	9.50	(5.88)	9.86	(4.33)	9.86	(5.41)
STAI	18.00	(3.49)	17.86	(4.80)	17.24	(4.67)	16.48	(4.08)
RSE	39.41	(4.63)	40.50	(5.01)	40.67	(7.98)	41.57	(7.95)
SCL	45.14	(32.85)	38.27	(31.20)	51.52	(49.09)	42.86	(44.12)
Wives								
DAS	82.91	(14.02)	90.86	(16.24)	83.38	(16.45)	84.57	(11.73)
ACQ	14.18	(5.31)	10.95	(5.83)	13.71	(4.61)	13.14	(5.76)
STAI	21.00	(4.86)	18.45	(4.34)	18.76	(6.49)	18.29	(3.42)
RSE	40.59	(7.82)	41.00	(7.25)	37.90	(5.58)	39.10	(5.30)
SCL	65.68	(59.30)	49.59	(42.31)	66.57	(44.65)	48.43	(29.13)

M = Mean
SD = Standard deviation

relationship measures, indicating that the SFMT group improved over time to a significantly greater extent compared to the waitlist group. The overall effect for time ($F_{2,40} = 3.51$, $p < .04$) was uninterpretable in light of the time × group interaction. No overall group differences across both assessment times were observed ($F_{2,40} = .66, p > .52$). Follow-up univariate analyses for husbands on the time × group interaction indicated an effect approaching significance on the DAS ($F_{1,41} = 3.86$, $p < .06$) and a significant effect on the ACQ ($F_{1,41} = 6.68, p < .01$). These results can be seen in Figures 12.1 and 12.2. The second repeated measures MANOVA analysis, targeting individual distress measures (STAI, RSE, SCL-90-R) demonstrated no significant time × group interaction ($F_{3,39} = .10, p > .96$), nor an overall effect for time ($F_{3,39} = 2.55, p > .07$) or group ($F_{3,39} = 1.12, p > .36$).

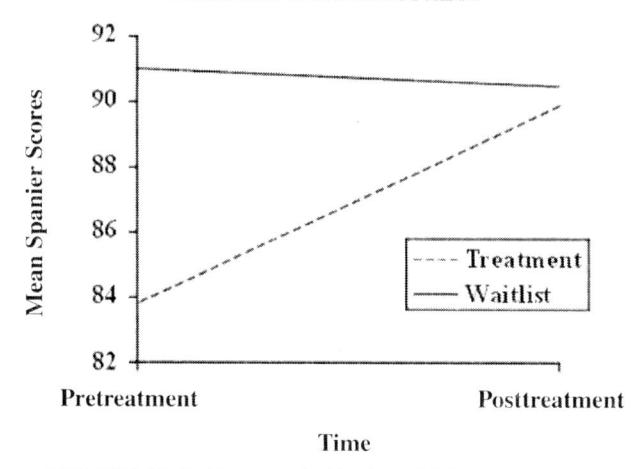

FIGURE 12.1. Changes in Husbands' Spanier Scores

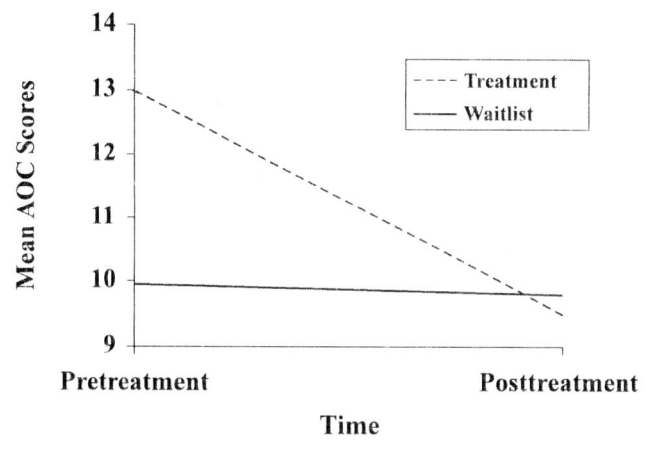

FIGURE 12.2. Changes in Husbands' Areas of Change Scores

When examined alone, wives did not demonstrate a significant multivariate group × time effect for the relationship measures ($F_{2,40} = 2.08, p > .14$). Wives did demonstrate a significant overall effect for time ($F_{2,40} = 4.04, p < .03$), indicating that both groups improved somewhat, but no overall group differences across both assessment times were observed ($F_{2,40} = .30, p > .75$). Wives also did not demonstrate a significant multivariate group × time effect for measures of individual distress ($F_{3,39} = 1.04, p > .39$); and no overall group differences across both assessment times were observed ($F_{3,39} = 1.21, p > .32$). These results can be seen in Figures 12.3 and 12.4.

Therapist Effects

A series of ANOVAS were computed in order to determine whether the outcome varied significantly across therapists. A series of one-way ANOVAs revealed no significant effects of individual therapist,

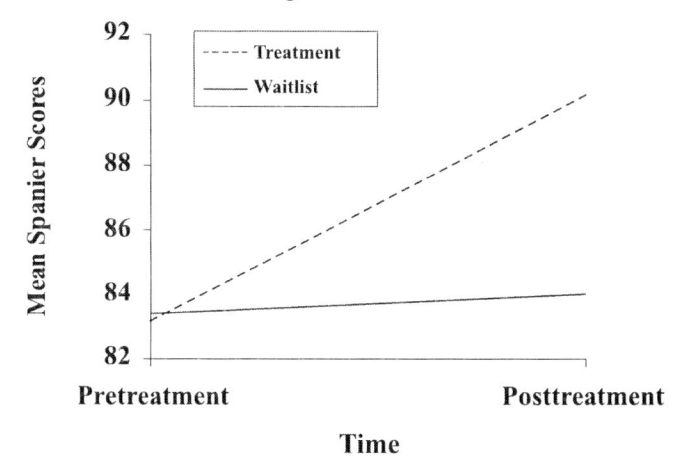

FIGURE 12.3. Changes in Wives' Spanier Scores

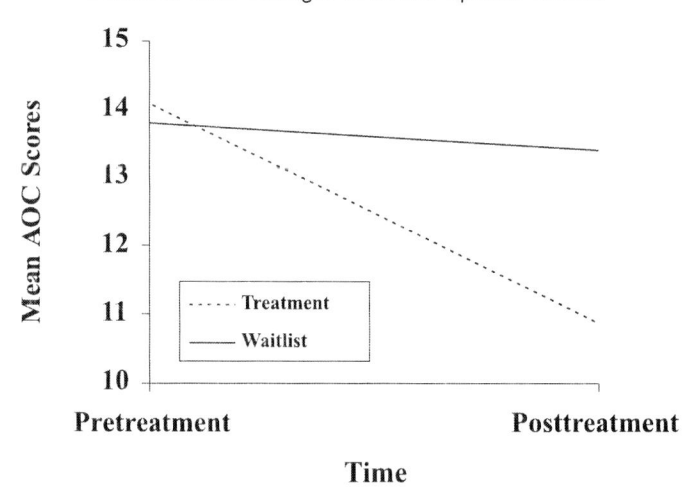

FIGURE 12.4. Changes in Wives' Areas of Change Scores

therapist marital status, or therapist gender. Analysis using two-tailed Pearson correlations revealed no significant correlations between therapist age or experience level and the DAS change scores.

Discussion

The results of the treatment waitlist-control comparison indicated that support-focused marital therapy, as administered by novice therapists in a university training clinic, is effective in increasing marital satisfaction. Relative to the waitlist-control group, the support-focused marital therapy group (husbands and wives combined) showed increases in marital satisfaction on two commonly accepted measures of marital satisfaction, the DAS and the ACQ.

When treatment waitlist-control comparisons were conducted separately for husbands and wives, a significant treatment effect on the ACQ for husbands was shown. The treatment effect for the DAS was in the predicted direction but did not reach statistically significant levels. The results for wives were also in the predicted direction; however, they also did not reach statistically significant levels. Given the relatively small sample size, and the fact that the study was conducted with novice therapists, these results are encouraging. They suggest that support-focused marital therapy has promise as a technique for increasing spousal marital satisfaction.

Interestingly, no comparable treatment waitlist-control differences were found on measures of individual distress. Although spouses showed significant reductions on measures of individual distress over time, they were comparable in the two groups. It would appear that couples in the present sample who responded to an advertisement for marital therapy were in crisis and that the mere passage of time was sufficient to reduce the distress associated with the marital crises. These results are in contrast to Snyder and Wills (1989) who found no change in a waitlist-control group on a measure of individual distress (the MMPI).

However, consistent with other studies (Dunn and Schwebel, 1995), the mere passage of time was not sufficient to improve marital satisfaction. For this to occur, a therapy intervention such as support-focused marital therapy appears to be required. In Dunn and Schwebel's review of the marital therapy outcome literature, it is suggested that the efficacy of marital therapy has been demonstrated and that now it is time to determine which approach to marital therapy is maximally effective with which type of marital distress. Ultimately, quite different marital therapies may be required to intervene effectively with the many different types of marital distress.

Although more research is clearly required, it is proposed that support-focused marital therapy will prove to be maximally effective with that subset of distressed marriages where the central issue is the wife's anger over issues of inequity and lack of support. Such couples appeared to be present in the current sample since wives presenting for treatment demonstrated more anger on the Spielberger Trait Anger Inventory and more dissatisfaction with their marriages on the ACQ. In such cases, if the husband has the resources to offer support, and the wife can learn to monitor and control her anger, support-focused marital therapy may be of value in increasing marital satisfaction. Informal observation of couples in the present sample suggests that when factors such as the presence of a DSM disorder (e.g., depressive disorder) or severe external stressors (e.g., financial problems) limit the husband's capacity to offer support, the treatment may be less effective. At present, attempts to identify those couples who might benefit most from support-focused marital therapy are under way.

Further research is also under way to deal with some of the limitations of the present research. This includes conducting a six-month follow-up of the couples treated in the present study to assess the stability of the treatment gains over time. It also includes defining the core therapist interventions in support-focused marital therapy and developing an objective scoring method to measure therapist adherence to the support-focused marital therapy treatment manual.

STUDY TWO: CORRELATIONS AMONG SUPPORT, ANGER, MARITAL SATISFACTION, AND CHANGE IN MARITAL SATISFACTION

Based on the importance placed on spousal support in support-focused marital therapy, it was predicted that prior to the onset of therapy, the degree to which a spouse perceived the partner as supportive would be related to that spouse's level of marital satisfaction. It was also predicted that increases in perceived partner support following therapy would be related to increases in spousal marital satisfaction.

It was predicted that prior to the onset of therapy the level of the partner's anger would be related to the level of the spouse's marital satisfaction. It was also predicted that reduction in the partner's level of anger would be related to increases in the spouse's level of marital satisfaction.

Perceived partner support was assessed using the Vinokur Social Support Scales later described. Marital satisfaction was assessed using the Spanier Dyadic Adjustment Scale, and anger was assessed using the Spielberger Trait Anger Inventory.

In order to test these hypotheses, a sample of 48 couples treated with support focused marital therapy was utilized. This sample included the 22 couples treated in the treatment waitlist-control study, 14 waitlist-control couples who were treated after a three-month waiting period, and 12 couples who were treated prior to the initiation of the treatment waitlist-control study.

Methods

Participants

The mean age of husbands in the sample was 46.9 and the range was 24-68; the mean age of wives was 44.7 and the range was 24-65. The average number of years married was 13.98 and the range was 1-43; 27.7 percent of the spouses had been married one or more times prior to the current marriage. With regard to education, 11.7 percent had doctoral degrees, 30.9 percent had master's degrees, 27.7 percent had college degrees, and 21.3 percent had high school degrees as their terminal degree. The mean total family income level was $102,000, and the range was $20,000 to $215,000. The average number of children living in the home was 1.47, and the range was 0-5; the average number of children not living in the home was .75, and the range was 0-5. Thirty-nine couples were white, one was Hispanic, and eight were interracial.

Measures

Vinokur Social Support Scales (Vinokur and Vinokur-Kaplan, 1990). The Vinokur scales consist of ten Likert-type items designed to assess the degree to which a spouse perceives the partner as supportive and the degree to which a spouse reports that he or she offers support to the partner. Only the perceived partner support scale was used in the present study. Internal reliability for the scales have been reported in the .85 to .92 range. Further reliability and validity evidence is presented in Vinokur, Schul, and Caplan (1987).

Therapists

Fourteen therapists were utilized in the present study. Four were beginning therapists who had less than two years of experience in a doctoral training program in clinical psychology and less than six months of supervised experience in psychotherapy. These therapists conducted the marital therapy as cotherapy teams. Eight therapists had more than two years of clinical training and more than six months of supervised psychotherapy training. Two therapists had doctoral degrees in clinical psychology. These ten therapists conducted the marital therapy sessions as solo therapists. All were considered novices at marital therapy. Therapist training included didactic instruction in use of the treatment manual, observation of training tapes, and weekly group supervision. Individual supervision was also conducted as needed. All supervision was provided by the first author who also reviewed all audiotapes of sessions to assess adherence to the manual. Each therapist was also required to fill out a seven-item "adherence to the manual" form after each session.

Procedure

All couples were administered the five outcome measures prior to session one. The Vinokur support scales were administered immediately before each treatment session. Since the Vinokur scales were employed after the project had begun, data were available for the last 33 cases. Prior to the beginning of session 12 the outcome measures were readministered and followed by the last treatment session.

Results

Correlates of Spouse Pretreatment Marital Satisfaction

Pearson product moment correlations were used to determine the relationship between perceived partner support and marital satisfaction on the

Spanier DAS assessed prior to session one. As predicted, the results indicated that, for wives, a significant positive relationship was found ($r = .67$, $n = 37$, $p < .001$). For husbands, a significant relationship was also found ($r = .42$, $n = 37$, $p < .01$).

Pearson correlations were also used to assess the relationship between the spouse's level of marital satisfaction and his or her partner's level of trait anger prior to session one. For husbands, as predicted, a significant relationship was found ($r = -.29$, $n = 48$, $p < .05$). For wives, no relationship was found ($r = .04$, $n = 48$, $p > .78$).

Changes in Perceived Partner Support

Mean scores and standard deviations on the Vinokur perceived partner support measure for sessions one, two, ten, and eleven are reported in Table 12.3. Change scores were determined by subtracting the mean of sessions ten and eleven from the mean of sessions one and two. For husbands, there was an increase in perceived partner support ($t(33) = 2.63$, $p < .02$). Wives also showed an increase in perceived partner support ($t(33) = 3.45$, $p < .002$).

Pretreatment/Posttreatment Change on the DAS and STAI

Pretreatment and posttreatment scores on the DAS and STAI scales can be seen in Table 12.4. For wives, these analyses showed significant pretest to posttest change on the Spanier DAS ($t(47) = -6.36$, $p < .001$). For husbands there was significant pretest to posttest change on the Spanier DAS ($t(47) = -5.26$, $p < .001$). For wives, on the Spielberger Trait Anger Inventory there was a significant reduction in anger ($t(45) = 4.01$, $p < .001$). For husbands, on the Spielberger Trait Anger Inventory there was also a significant reduction in anger ($t(46) = 2.18$, $p < .03$).

Correlates of Change in Marital Satisfaction

Pearson correlation coefficients were used to determine if increases in marital satisfaction on the DAS were correlated with increases in perceived partner support. The results indicated that, for wives, as predicted, a significant relationship was found ($r = .72$, $n = 32$, $p < .001$). For husbands, no relationship was found ($r = .14$, $n = 32$, $p > .42$).

TABLE 12.3. Means and Standard Deviations on Vinokur Perceived Partner Support Scale

	Perceived Partner Support	
	M	(SD)
Husbands		
Session One	2.71	(.54)
Session Two	2.73	(.49)
Session Ten	2.93	(.47)
Session Eleven	3.03	(.57)
Wives		
Session One	2.70	(.56)
Session Two	2.88	(.52)
Session Ten	3.02	(.58)
Session Eleven	3.08	(.48)

M = Mean
SD = Standard deviation

TABLE 12.4. Means and Standard Deviations DAS and STAI

	DAS		STAI	
	M	(SD)	M	(SD)
Husbands				
Pretreatment	85.95	(16.00)	17.59	(3.50)
Posttreatment	97.30	(13.91)	16.26	(3.53)
Wives				
Pretreatment	81.60	(13.50)	20.79	(5.75)
Posttreatment	93.86	(17.77)	19.20	(4.68)

M = Mean
SD = Standard deviation

Pearson coefficients were also used to determine if increases on the Spanier DAS were correlated with decreases in partner anger. The results indicated that, for husbands, a significant relationship was found ($r = .38$, $n = 48$, $p < .01$). For wives, no relationship was found ($r = .19$, $n = 48$, $p > .18$).

Discussion

According to the present analysis, many marital problems begin when wives perceive lack of husband support and begin to make negative attributions ("my husband is intentionally disregarding"), begin to experience anger, and subsequently engage in negative behavior (accusations and criticism) in an attempt to correct the perceived injustice. The results of study one did support the notion that wives were more dissatisfied with their marriages and angrier than their husbands. Since their experience of anger and subsequent negative behavior goes against their socialization, wives become their own "worst enemies," thus adding to their psychological distress (Sharkin, 1993).

The results confirm the hypothesis that perceived support is a particularly crucial dimension for wives. Wives' pretreatment levels of marital satisfaction were related to the level of support they perceived receiving from their husbands. Similarly, after treatment, wives who experienced higher levels of perceived husband support reported higher levels of marital satisfaction. Wives appear to monitor their husbands' behavior for evidence of support. It is a key mechanism in understanding both their initial level of marital satisfaction and their increased marital satisfaction following treatment.

For husbands, support appears to be less significant in understanding their experience of marital satisfaction. Although their pretreatment levels of perceived wife support were related to their pretreatment level of marital satisfaction, change in the level of perceived wife support was not related to a change in their level of marital satisfaction following therapy. Consistent with the approach of support-focused marital therapy, the results suggest that what appears more relevant to husbands is the level of their wives' anger. It was related to the husbands' initial level of marital satisfaction, and the degree of reduction in the level of wives' anger was related to increases in husbands' marital satisfaction following treatment.

It is proposed that over time, husbands become highly sensitized to their wives' anger and monitor their wives closely for the presence of anger. Whereas distressed wives seeking marital therapy are highly sensitized to the support dimension, husbands seeking marital therapy are highly sensitized to the anger dimension.

Afterword

The author's goal in writing this book was to describe support-focused marital therapy, a new way of conceptualizing distressed marriages and intervening to increase marital satisfaction. In the first section, it was proposed that social support is a key concept in understanding marriage. The spouse's perception that the partner is *not* supportive is central to understanding the process of marital deterioration. It was suggested that as a result of lack of perceived support, destructive interactional patterns emerge in five areas of marriage: lack of instrumental and emotional support, triangulation, derogation and negative escalation, communication avoidance, and intimacy avoidance.

It was emphasized that if the therapist can make an emotional connection with each spouse, help each spouse understand the perspective and often painful position of the partner, present the destructive interactional pattern to the couple, assign homework directed at altering the destructive pattern, identify and overcome obstacles to homework completion, and follow through, constructive change will occur, which will ultimately result in increased marital satisfaction.

In the second section, a manual was presented that contains a detailed description of how the therapist accomplishes the previously mentioned tasks. The third section presented a session-by-session case history that allows the reader to get a sense of how support-focused marital therapy is implemented over a course of treatment, and the final section discussed the outcome data. Using novice therapists, it was demonstrated that support-focused marital therapy was superior to a waitlist-control group in increasing marital satisfaction. It was also demonstrated that greater perceived husband support appears more central to the wife's experience of marital satisfaction, whereas decreased wife anger is more central to the husband's experience of marital satisfaction.

Marital distress is a highly complex process. It is doubtful that any single way of conceptualizing troubled marriages will prove useful with all distressed couples, nor will there be any single treatment that will be effective with all distressed couples. It is the author's hope that after reading this text the therapist will have new and useful ways of thinking about distressed couples. Hopefully, when couples that seem to be a good fit for support-focused marital therapy present themselves, the therapist will consider the interventions described in this text.

References

Antonucci, T.C. and Akiyama, H. (1987). An examination of sex differences in social support among older men and women. *Sex Roles, 17,* 737-749.

Barnett, L. and Nietzel, G. (1979). Relationship of instrumental and affectional behaviors and self-esteem to marital satisfaction in distressed and non-distressed couples. *Journal of Consulting and Clinical Psychology, 47,* 946-957.

Belle, D. (1982). The stress of caring: Women as providers of social support. In L. Goldberger and S. Breznitz (Eds.), *Handbook of stress: Theoretical and clinical aspects.* New York: Free Press.

Bird, C. (1999). Gender, household labor, and psychological distress: The impact of the amount and division of housework. *Journal of Health and Social Behavior, 40,* 32-45.

Bloch, H.R. (1991). *Medieval misogyny and the invention of Western romantic love.* Chicago: University of Chicago Press.

Bordin, E. (1979). The generality of the psychoanalytic concept of the working alliance. *Psychotherapy: Theory, Research, and Practice, 16,* 252-260.

Bradbury, T. and Fincham, F. (1990). Attributions in marriage: Review and critique. *Psychological Bulletin, 107,* 3-33.

Bradbury, T., Fincham, F., Beach, S., and Nelson, G. (1996). Attributions and behavior in functional and dysfunctional marriages. *Journal of Consulting and Clinical Psychology, 64,* 569-576.

Brunstein, J.C., Dangelmayer, G., and Schultheiss, O.C. (1996). Personal goals and social support in close relationships: Effects of relationship mood and marital satisfaction. *Journal of Personality and Social Psychology, 71,* 1006-1019.

Cobb, S. (1976). Social support as a moderator of life stress. *Psychosomatic Medicine, 38,* 300-314.

Corcoran, K. and Fischer, J. (1987). *Measures for clinical practice: A sourcebook.* New York: Free Press.

Cutrona, C. (1996). *Social support in couples.* Thousand Oaks, CA: Sage.

Depner, C.E. and Ingersoll-Dayton, B. (1985). Conjugal support patterns in later life. *Journal of Gerontology, 40,* 761-766.

Derogatis, L.R. (1989). *Description and bibliography for the SCL-90-R and other instruments of the psychopathology rating scale series.* Riverwood, MD: Clinical Psychometric Research, Inc.

DuBois, D.L., Felner, R.D., Sherman, M.D., and Bull, C.A. (1994). Socioenvironmental experiences, self-esteem, and emotional/behavioral problems in early adolescence. *American Journal of Community Psychology, 22,* 371-397.

Dunn, R. and Schwebel, A. (1995). Meta-analytic review of marital therapy outcome research. *Journal of Family Psychology, 9,* 58-68.

Franks, M.M. and Stephens, M.A. (1996) Social support in the context of caregiving: Husbands' provision of support to wives involved in parental care. *Journal of Gerontology, 51,* 43-52.

Gottman, J. (1990). How marriages change. In G. Patterson (Ed.), *Depression and aggression in family interaction.* Hillsdale, NJ: Lawrence Erlbaum.

Gottman, J. M. (1994). *What predicts divorce? The relationship between marital processes and marital outcomes.* Hillsdale, NJ: Lawrence Erlbaum Associates.

Greenstein, T. (2000). Economic dependence, gender, and the division of labor in the home: A replication and extension. *Journal of Marriage and the Family, 62,* 322-335.

Heavey, C., Layne, C., and Christensen, A. (1993). Gender and conflict structure in marital interaction: A replication and extension. *Journal of Consulting and Clinical, 61*(1), 16-27.

Heim, S. and Snyder, D. (1991). Predicting depression from marital distress and attributional processes. *Journal of Marital and Family Therapy, 17*(1), 67-72.

Huston, T. (2000). The social ecology of marriage and other intimate unions. *Journal of Marriage and the Family, 62,* 298-320.

Ingledew, D.K., Hardy, L., and Cooper, C.L. (1997). Do resources buffer coping and does coping buffer stress? An organizational study with longitudinal aspects and control for negative affectivity. *Journal of Occupational Health Psychology, 2,* 118-133.

Jacobson, N.S. and Margolin, G. (1979). *Marital therapy: Strategies based on social learning and behavioral exchange principles.* New York: Brunner/Mazel.

Johnson, S. and Greenberg, L. (1985). Emotionally focused couples therapy: An outcome study. *Journal of Marital and Family Therapy, 11,* 313-317.

Johnson, S. and Talitman, E. (1997). Predictors of success in emotionally focused marital therapy. *Journal of Marital and Family Therapy, 23,* 135-152.

Jordan, J.V. (1991). *Women's growth in connection.* New York: Guilford.

Kawash, G. and Lozeluk, L. (1990). Self-esteem in early adolescence as a function of position within Olson's circumplex model of marital and family systems. *Social Behavior and Personality, 18,* 189-196.

Kayser, K. (1993). *When love dies: The process of marital disaffection.* New York: Guilford.

Lackovic, Grgin, K., Dekovic, M., Milosavljevic, B., Cvek-Sorie, I., and Opacic, G. (1996). Social support and self-esteem in unemployed university graduates. *Adolescence, 31,* 701-707.

Margolin, G. and Fernandez, V. (1983). Other marriage and family questionnaires. In E. Filsinger (Ed.), *Marriage and family assessment: A sourcebook for family therapy.* Beverly Hills, CA: Sage.

McGrath, E., Keita, G.P., Strickland, B.R., and Russo, N.F. (1990). *Women and depression.* Washington, DC: American Psychological Association.

Murstein, B. and Beck, G. (1972). Person perception, marriage adjustment, and social desirability. *Journal of Consulting and Clinical Psychology, 39,* 396-403.

Notarius, C., Benson, P., Sloan, D., Vanzetti, N., and Hornyak, L. (1989). Exploring the interface between perception and behavior: An analysis of marital interaction in distressed and non-distressed couples. *Behavior Assessment, 11*, 39-64.

Ozment, S.E. (1983). *When fathers ruled: Family life in reformation Europe*. Cambridge, MA: Harvard University Press.

Pistrang, N. and Barker, C. (1995). The relationship in psychological response to breast cancer. *Social Science and Medicine, 40*, 789-797.

Pretty, G.M.H., Conroy, C., Dugay, J. Fowler, K., and Williams, D. (1996). Sense of community and its relevance to adolescents of all ages. *Journal of Community Psychology, 11*, 1-24.

Rosenberg, M. (1965). *Society and the adolescent self-image*. Princeton, NJ: Princeton University Press.

Rosenberg, M. (1989). *Society and the adolescent self-image*. Middletown, CT: Wesleyan University Press.

Rosenfield, L.B. and Richman, J.M. (1997). Developing effective social support: Team building and the social support process. *Journal of Applied Sport Psychology, 9*, 133-153.

Sharkin, B.S. (1993). Anger and gender: Theory, research, and implications. *Journal of Counseling and Development, 71*, 386-389.

Short, J.L., Sandler, I.N., and Roosa, M.W. (1991). Adolescents' perception of social support: Esteem enhancement and self-esteem threat. Poster presented at the Third Biennial Conference on Community Research and Action, Tempe, AZ.

Snyder, D.K. and Wills, R.M. (1989). Behavioral versus insight-oriented marital therapy. *Journal of Consulting and Clinical Psychology, 57*, 39-46.

Spanier, G.B. (1976). Measuring dyadic adjustment: New scales for assessing the quality of marriage and similiar dyads. *Journal of Marriage and the Family, 38*, 15-28.

Spielberger, C.D., Jacobs, G.A., Russell, S., and Crane, R.J. (1983). Assessment of anger: The state-trait anger scale. In L.N. Butcher and C.D. Spielberger (Eds.), *Advances in personality assessment*, Volume 2 (pp. 161-189). Hillsdale, NJ: Lawrence Erlbaum Associates.

Steiner, A., Raube, K., Stuck, A.E., Aronow, H.U., Draper, D., Rubenstein, L.Z., and Beck, J.C. (1996). Measuring psychological aspects of well-being in older community residents: Performance of four short scales. *Gerontologist, 36*, 54-62.

Steptoe, A., Wardle, J., Pollard, T.M., and Canaan, L. (1996). Stress, social support, and health-related behavior: A study of smoking, alcohol consumption, and physical exercise. *Journal of Psychosomatic Research, 41*, 171-180.

Tyler, P. and Cushway, D. (1995). Stress in nurses: The effects of coping and social support. *Stress Medicine, 11*, 243-251.

Vinokur, A.D., Price, R.H., and Caplan, R.D. (1996). Hard times and hurtful partners: How financial strain affects depression and relationship satisfaction of unemployed persons and their spouses. *Journal of Personality and Social Psychology, 71*, 166-179.

Vinokur, A.D., Schul, Y., and Caplan, R.D. (1987). Determinants of perceived social support: Interpersonal transactions, personal outlook, and transient affective states. *Journal of Personality and Social Psychology, 53*, 1137-1145.

Vinokur, A.D. and Vinokur-Kaplan, D. (1990). "In sickness and in health": Patterns of social support and undermining in older married couples. *Journal of Aging and Health, 2,* 215-241.

Weinberger, J. (1995). Common factors aren't so common: The common factors dilemma. *Clinical Psychology: Science and Practice,* 45-69.

Weiss, R.L., Hops, H., and Patterson, G.R. (1973). A framework for conceptualizing marital conflict, a technology for altering it, some data for evaluating it. In L.A. Hamerlynck, L.C. Handy, and E.J. Mash (Eds.), *Behavior change: Methodology, concepts, and practice.* Champaign, IL: Research Press.

Weissman, M. (1987). Advances in psychiatric epidemiology: Rates and risks for major depression. *American Journal of Public Health, 77,* 445-451.

Zachariah, R. (1996). Predictors of psychological well-being of women during pregnancy: Relapse and extension. *Journal of Social Behavior and Personality, 11,* 127-140.

Index

ACQ, 138-139
Affection, encouraging, 109-111
Anger, correlations among support, marital satisfaction, and, 147
    discussion, 152-153
    methods, 148-149
    results, 149-152
Anger management, 83-99
    emotional obstacles to, and inhibition of criticism
        dealing with Paul's belief that Jane should change, 95
        depersonalizing put-downs, 98
        following up, 99
        probing for inhibition of angry criticism, 99
        reframing angry outbursts as attempt to be heard, 95-96
        reframing belief that angry criticism is justified, 96
        reframing belief that partner is oversensitive and should change, 97
    framing issue as, 91-92
    inappropriate, as function of deterioration
        assigning tasks, 95
        door slamming and plate throwing, 93-94
        "no excuse for loss of control" reframe, 92-93
        problem solving, 94
        using here and now to point out derogation, 94-95
    therapist as gatekeeper, 84-90
Areas of Change Questionnaire (ACQ), 138-139
Assignments
    coordinated homework, 46-47, 77
    detriangulation, 78

Assignments *(continued)*
    following up on
        focusing on successful, 52-55
        processing failures to carry out, 55-57
        remaining objective, 52
    "monitor and edit your anger," 45
    obstacles to, 47-48
    unilateral, 77
    "what can I do to help?", 43-44

Communication
    direct, 101, 105-108
    indirect, 8, 101-102
Communication avoidance
    describing pattern of, 102-104
    obstacles to direct communication
        dealing with conflict avoidance by problem solving, 106
        dealing with fear of loss of control, 105-106
        depersonalizing partner's anger, 105
        following up with assignments, 107-108
        reframing fear of partner's anger, 105
        using here and now of session to encourage direct communication, 106-107
Companionship
    anticipating obstacles to, 112
    encouraging, 111-114
    processing attempts at, 112-114
    understanding each spouse's desire for, 111-112
Conflict avoidance, indirect communication and, 101-102

161

DAS, 138
Derogation, 7-8, 83-99
 therapist as gatekeeper, 84-90
 using here and now to point out, 94-95
Direct communication, 101, 105-108
Dismissive attitude pattern, 57-58
Downward questions, 16-17
Dyadic Adjustment Scale (DAS), 138

Emotional support, 2, 6-7
Empathic probing, 10, 13
 downward questions, 16-17
 outward questions, 15-16
Empathy, of therapist, 13-14
Esteem support, 2

Gender, and social support, 4-5

Hobby triangle
 brainstorming and problem solving, 78-79
 coordinated homework assignments, 77
 dealing with emotional obstacles to detriangulating, 79-81
 describing the pattern, 78
 detriangulation assignments, 78
 probing for painful affect and presenting triangular pattern, 77-78
 triangulation based on real avoidance of partner, 81-82
 unilateral assignments, 77

Indirect communication, 8, 101-102
Informational support, 2
Instrumental support, 2, 6-7

Marital distress
 as highly complex process, 155-156

Marital distress *(continued)*
 patterns of
  derogation and negative escalation, 7-8
  indirect communication, 8
  lack of emotional and instrumental support, 6-7
  loss of companionship, affection and intimacy, 9
  triangulation, 7
Marital satisfaction, correlations among support, anger, and, 147
 discussion, 152-153
 methods, 148-149
 results, 149-152
Marital therapy. *See* Support-focused marital therapy
Marriage
 mutual support in, 4-5
 stress in contemporary, 1

Negative escalation, 7-8, 83-99
 teaching couples to avoid, 90-91
 therapist as gatekeeper, 84-90
Nonsexual touching, 114-115

Outward questions, 15-16

Parenting triangle, 69-74
 assessment of child or adolescent, 71
 assessment of parenting, 71-72
 identifying objectionable behavior, 70
 probing for inner experience of each spouse, 70-71
Partner differences and limitations
 accepting gender differences, 124-125
 differences as irritant, 121-122
 learning to accept
  bragging, 124
  fears, 123
  introversion, 122

Index

Partner differences and limitations, learning to accept *(continued)*
    rigidity, 123
    somatization, 123-124
Patterns
    of marital distress, 6-9
    offering preliminary observations about, 21-22
    presenting Mary and Pete's, 33-35
    triangulation, 69-82
Processing
    of conflicts and interactions, 27-28
    Mary and Pete's conflict, 28
        working with Mary, 29-31
        working with Pete, 31-33

Rosenberg Self-Esteem Inventory (RSE), 139

Sam and Diane case study
    sessions one through eighteen, 127-135
    subsequent sessions, 135
SCL-90-R, 139
Self-esteem, social support and, 3
Sexual intimacy, 115-119
Shapo, Jacqueline Raznik, 137
Social support. *See also* Support
    literature on
        gender and support, 4-5
        marital therapy and support, 5-6
        social undermining and marital dissatisfaction, 3-4
        support and self-esteem, 3
        support and well-being, 2-3
    types of, 2
Social undermining, 3-4
Spielberger Trait Anger Inventory (STAI), 139
STAI, 139
Support. *See also* Social support
    correlations among anger, marital satisfaction, and, 147
        discussion, 152-153
        methods, 148-149
        results, 149-152

Support *(continued)*
    emotional, 2, 6-7
    esteem, 2
    informational, 2
    instrumental, 2, 6-7
    reframing obstacles to providing
        defensiveness, 51
        fear of being controlled, 49-50
        fear of being overburdened, 50
        fear of disappointment, 51
        inertia and resistance to change, 48-49
    role of, 1-12
        literature on social support, 2-6
        overwhelmed spouses and, 1-2
        patterns of marital distress, 6-9
    social, 2
Support lists, 61-66
Support-focused marital therapy, 2
    administrative matters, 25
    affectionate behavior, encouraging, 109-111
    anger management
        emotional obstacles and inhibition of criticism, 95-99
        framing issue as, 91-92
        inappropriate, as function of marital deterioration, 92-95
        therapist as gatekeeper, 84-90
    assessing effectiveness of
        correlations among support, anger, and marital satisfaction, 147-153
        support-focused marital therapy waitlist control comparison, 137-147
    assignments
        coordinated homework assignment, 46-47
        following up on, 52-57
        "monitor and edit your anger" assignment, 45
        providing rationale for helping, 44-45
        understanding and reframing inner emotional obstacles to, 47-48
        "what can I do to help?" assignment, 43-44

Support-focused marital therapy *(continued)*
  behavioral tasks, 11-12
  communication avoidance
    describing pattern of, 102-104
    direct communication, 101
    indirect communication and conflict avoidance, 101-102
    obstacles to direct communication, 105-108
  companionship, encouraging, 111-114
  derogation, 83-99
    therapist as gatekeeper, 84-90
    using here and now to point out, 94-95
  developmental history, 39-40
  dismissive attitude pattern, 57-58
  empathic probing, 10, 13, 15-17
  establishing therapeutic alliance, 10
    describing spouses' roles, 22-23
    describing therapist's role, 22
    determining spouses' goals for therapy, 20-21
    discussing commitment, 23
    offering preliminary observations about problems and patterns, 21-22
    winning cooperation of reluctant spouse, 23-24
  following up on assignments, 52-57
  increasing emotional connection, 37-38
  individual sessions, 37-41
  keeping support issue on table and monitoring progress, 67
  marital history, 38-39
  negative escalation, 83-99
    teaching couples to avoid, 90-91
    therapist as gatekeeper, 84-90
  as new way of conceptualizing and intervening in distressed marriages, 155-156
  nonsexual touching, encouraging, 114-115
  partner differences and limitations, 121-125
    accepting gender differences, 124-125

Support-focused marital therapy, partner differences and limitations *(continued)*
    differences as irritant, 121-122
    learning to accept, 122-124
  preparing couple for individual therapy, 35-36
  processing conflicts and presenting patterns, 27-36
    Mary and Pete's conflict, 28-33
    Mary and Pete's pattern, 33-35
    processing conflicts and interactions, 27-28
  providing new information about partner and relationship, 11
  reframing obstacles to providing support
    defensiveness, 51
    fear of being controlled, 49-50
    fear of being overburdened, 50
    fear of disappointment, 51
    inertia and resistance to change, 48-49
  reorienting couple after individual therapy, 40-41
  sexual intimacy, encouraging, 115-119
  and social support, 5-6
  support lists
    Mary, 62-64
    Pete, 64-66
  therapist as relationship instructor, 35
  therapist's goals, 13, 27, 37
  triangulation patterns
    parenting triangle, 69-76
    work/hobby triangle, 76-82
  unilateral attempt to prevail pattern, 58-61
  working empathically with spouses
    asking partner to identify problems, 19
    clarifying and holding spouses' incompatible views, 18-19
    concrete examples, 15
    conveying spouse's experience to partner, 17
    downward questions, 16-17

Support-focused marital therapy,
        working empathically with
        spouses *(continued)*
    eliciting and demonstrating equal
        respect for spouse's point
        of view, 18
    outward questions, 15-16
    therapist as gatekeeper, 18
Support-focused marital therapy
        waitlist-control comparison
    discussion, 146-147
    method
        measures, 138-139
        participants, 138
        procedure, 140
        therapists, 140
    results
        change as function of treatment,
            141-142
        demographic variables, 140-141
        pretreatment measures, 141
        randomization, 140
        separate analysis for husbands
            and wives, 142-145
        therapist effects, 145-146

Therapeutic alliance, establishing, 10,
        20-22
Therapists
    empathy of, 13-14
    as gatekeepers, 18
        calming derogatory system with
            empathic probing, 88-90
        tools for, 84-87
Triangulation, 7
    parenting triangle
        assessment of child or
            adolescent, 71
        assessment of parenting, 71-72
        brainstorming, 74-75
        describing pattern, 72-74
        follow-up, 75-76
        identifying objectionable
            behavior, 70
        probing for obstacles, 75-76

Triangulation, parenting triangle
        (continued)
    probing inner experience of each
        spouse, 70-71
    work/hobby triangle
        brainstorming and problem
            solving, 78-79
        coordinated homework
            assignments, 77
        describing the pattern, 78
        detriangulation assignments, 78
        probing for obstacles and
            following through, 79
        probing for painful affect and
            presenting triangular pattern,
            77-78
        triangulation based on real
            avoidance of partner, 81-82
        unilateral assignments, 77

Unilateral attempt to prevail pattern,
        58-61

Vinokur Social Support Scales,
        148-149

Well-being, social support and, 2-3
Work triangle
    brainstorming and problem solving,
        78-79
    coordinated homework assignments,
        77
    describing the pattern, 78
    detriangulation assignments, 78
    probing for obstacles and following
        through, 79
    probing for painful affect and
        presenting triangular pattern,
        77-78
    triangulation based on real
        avoidance of partner, 81-82
    unilateral assignments, 77

SPECIAL 25%-OFF DISCOUNT!
Order a copy of this book with this form or online at:
http://www.haworthpressinc.com/store/product.asp?sku=4747

TREATING MARITAL STRESS
Support-Based Approaches

_____ in hardbound at $37.46 (regularly $49.95) (ISBN: 0-7890-1631-1)

_____ in softbound at $18.71 (regularly $24.95) (ISBN: 0-7890-1632-X)

Or order online and use Code HEC25 in the shopping cart.

COST OF BOOKS_____	☐ **BILL ME LATER:** ($5 service charge will be added)
OUTSIDE USA/CANADA/ MEXICO: ADD 20%_____	(Bill-me option is good on US/Canada/Mexico orders only; not good to jobbers, wholesalers, or subscription agencies.)
POSTAGE & HANDLING_____ (US: $4.00 for first book & $1.50 for each additional book) Outside US: $5.00 for first book & $2.00 for each additional book)	☐ Check here if billing address is different from shipping address and attach purchase order and billing address information.
	Signature_____
SUBTOTAL_____	☐ **PAYMENT ENCLOSED:** $_____
in Canada: add 7% GST_____	☐ **PLEASE CHARGE TO MY CREDIT CARD.**
STATE TAX_____ (NY, OH & MIN residents, please add appropriate local sales tax)	☐ Visa ☐ MasterCard ☐ AmEx ☐ Discover ☐ Diner's Club ☐ Eurocard ☐ JCB
	Account #_____
FINAL TOTAL_____ (If paying in Canadian funds, convert using the current exchange rate. UNESCO coupons welcome.)	Exp. Date_____
	Signature_____

Prices in US dollars and subject to change without notice.

NAME_____
INSTITUTION_____
ADDRESS_____
CITY_____
STATE/ZIP_____
COUNTRY_____ COUNTY (NY residents only)_____
TEL_____ FAX_____
E-MAIL_____

May we use your e-mail address for confirmations and other types of information? ☐ Yes ☐ No
We appreciate receiving your e-mail address and fax number. Haworth would like to e-mail or fax special discount offers to you, as a preferred customer. **We will never share, rent, or exchange your e-mail address or fax number.** We regard such actions as an invasion of your privacy.

Order From Your Local Bookstore or Directly From
The Haworth Press, Inc.
10 Alice Street, Binghamton, New York 13904-1580 • USA
TELEPHONE: 1-800-HAWORTH (1-800-429-6784) / Outside US/Canada: (607) 722-5857
FAX: 1-800-895-0582 / Outside US/Canada: (607) 722-6362
E-mailto: getinfo@haworthpressinc.com
PLEASE PHOTOCOPY THIS FORM FOR YOUR PERSONAL USE.
http://www.HaworthPress.com   BOF02